TEST YOUR IN-LAW ETIQUETTE

1. You're back from your honeymoon approximately 14 mintues when the phone rings. It's your mother-in-law wondering when you are going to start having kids. You reply
   a. As soon as we can.
   b. It's none of your damn business!
   c. Didn't we tell you? The baby's due in six months.

2. There are 39 in-laws on your Christmas and Chanukah list. You decide to
   a. Buy 39 personalized gifts.
   b. Get everyone tickets to a Yankees game.
   c. Have one of you schedule elective surgery for the last week in December.

3. You've found the house of your dreams. Your in-laws offer to give you the $30,000 down payment. You
   a. Decline the offer graciously, insisting that you want to make it on your own.
   b. Decline the offer, knowing that if you accept, you'll owe them for the rest of your lives.
   c. Forget the eternal guilt—take the money and run.

No matter what the situation—never, ever let your in-laws gain the upper hand. Go for shock value, cheap sympathy, and your own personal gain. This train of thought will lead to a long-lasting, tolerable relationship.

♥ THE UNOFFICIAL NEWLYWEDS' HANDBOOK ♥

ALEXIS MAGNER MILLER & GEORGE W. MILLER are both writers for the *Providence Journal Bulletin*, where Alexis also has a weekly feature column in which she writes about her favorite topic—herself. The Millers live in Pascoag, Rhode Island, with their daughters, Rachel and Katy, and their dog, Kirby.

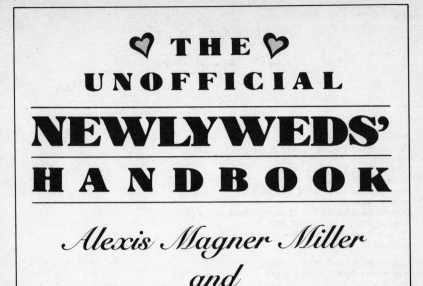

♥ THE ♥
UNOFFICIAL
NEWLYWEDS'
HANDBOOK

Alexis Magner Miller
and
George W. Miller

Illustrations by Frank Caswell

A PLUME BOOK

To Rachel and Katy
Love you always

PLUME
Published by the Penguin Group
Penguin Books USA Inc., 375 Hudson Street,
New York, New York 10014, U.S.A.
Penguin Books Ltd, 27 Wrights Lane,
London W8 5TZ, England
Penguin Books Australia Ltd, Ringwood,
Victoria, Australia
Penguin Books Canada Ltd, 10 Alcorn Avenue,
Toronto, Ontario, Canada M4V 3B2
Penguin Books (N.Z.) Ltd, 182–190 Wairau Road,
Auckland 10, New Zealand

Penguin Books Ltd, Registered Offices:
Harmondsworth, Middlesex, England

First published by Plume,
an imprint of New American Library,
a division of Penguin Books USA Inc.

First Printing, September, 1991
10 9 8 7 6 5 4 3 2 1

REGISTERED TRADEMARK—MARCA REGISTRADA

LIBRARY OF CONGRESS CATALOGING-IN-PUBLICATION DATA
Miller, Alexis Magner.
    The unofficial newlyweds' handbook / Alexis Magner Miller and
George W. Miller : illustrations by Frank Caswell.
        p.   cm.
    ISBN 0-452-25581-5
    1. Marriage—Humor. 2. Married people—Humor. I. Miller, George
W. (George Wayne), 1954–   . II. Title.
PN6231.M3M54   1991
818'.5401—dc20   91-10692
                                                        CIP

Printed in the United States of America
Set in Clearface and Snell Roundhand Script

Contents

♥ INTRODUCTION ♥

♥ CHAPTER 1 ♥

Prenuptials 11

With any luck, you'll read this before walking down
the aisle. Good. You may not change your mind,
but you may still have time to find a band that refuses
to play the hully-gully.

♥ CHAPTER 2 ♥

*The Perfect(?)
Honeymoon* 23

Romantic dinners, lazy days, moonlit nights. This sort of
honeymoon exists in airline ads—the very same air-
lines that will ruin your trip by losing your
luggage.

♥ CHAPTER 3 ♥

Talk's Not Cheap 33

Married communication is an oxymoron. That should
tell you something, but it won't.

♥ CHAPTER 4 ♥

Housekeeping 45

Before, you never even noticed Behind the Toilet.
Now you'll argue over who's going to clean it. At
least be creative in presenting your case.

♥ CHAPTER 5 ♥

In-Laws 57

Regrettably, America does not operate under the
Islamic code of justice. That doesn't mean there
aren't ways to make your in-laws feel as bad as they
make you feel.

♥ CHAPTER 6 ♥

Pets 67

Your pet, like your mother, will hate the person you
marry. The best compromise may be dumping the
cats and dogs and getting a rabbit, which, when no
longer cuddly, can be eaten.

♥ CHAPTER 7 ♥

Finances 75

You will never again have enough money. This is all
you need to know about finances.

♥ CHAPTER 8 ♥

Leisure Activities 87

And you will never again agree on how to spend your
free time. This is all you need to know about
leisure activities.

♥ CHAPTER 9 ♥

Romance 97

Romeo and Juliet, arguably the most romantic couple
of all time, died in their teens. You may think
you'll still feel amorous at thirty. Good luck.

♥ CHAPTER 10 ♥

The Honeymoon's Over 107

Unless you planned on the Poconos, in which case
it was over before it began, your honeymoon will last
until you get the American Express bill.

Author's Note

We had a lot of help and encourage-
ment. To Roger and Mary: thanks for
watching the kids. To Chris Schelling:
thanks for thinking of us. And to Kay
McCauley: thanks for everything.

Introduction

So you meet and date and fall in love. After a while, you decide to spend the rest of your lives together. You decide to get married. It's a testament to your undying love, an affirmation of your status as soul mates, and, just possibly, the stupidest thing you'll ever do.

You don't know that yet, any more than you really know the first thing about the person you're marrying.

As newlyweds, you'll find out.

You'll learn, for example, that he calls his mother every day. You'll learn that she sleeps with her cat. That he insists on

He said: "Let's move in together . . ."

She heard: "Let's get married with a big wedding . . . with lots of guests and . . ."

And so they were married in a big wedding with . . .

arranging the spices in alphabetical order and gets crazy when they're not. That she won't make a move on anything, including you, without consulting her horoscope. That he wants his ship in a bottle, which he made in summer camp, displayed on the mantel. That she considers cows the ultimate decorating motif.

By anticipating some of the pitfalls of the first year of marriage, you may be able to avoid them. But it's unlikely.

Which is why there are package stores and cable TV.

Chapter 1

Prenuptials

She has her diamond. He's told the guys at work. There's been a shower and an announcement in the local paper. You've gotten engaged and now you have to get down to the nitty-gritty: you have to have your wedding.

Do yourselves a favor:

Don't.

Plan to elope, but tell no one, of course, of your true intent. Plunge ahead with your plans. Draw up the guest list. Order the invitations. Hire the caterer. Then, in the final few days, when things start to get really serious—deciding whether the gift you'll get from your third cousin in Dubuque is worth the price of having such a horse's ass at your wedding, for example—skip town. This will be infinitely easier than enduring your own wedding day, as anyone who's been through it will tell you.

Please understand, however, how much elopement will infuriate both sets of parents; in fact, disgust at your shocking and insensitive behavior— namely, looking out for *your* interests—may be the only point on which your future in-laws will ever agree. Parents can be useful, and not only for picking up the tab for your reception, which, even if you hold it at BJ's Bowlarama, will cost more than the gross national product of any small foreign nation. If you expect ever to be able to borrow a down payment for a house, you probably will cast personal comfort and sanity aside and choose to go ahead with the Big Day. That means you have to start planning. Now. Planning will consume your every waking hour, cause endless fights, and alienate at least one branch of the family.

This grief will pale by comparison to the aggravation of the actual wedding day, as you will discover soon enough.

Setting a Date

This is not as easy as it sounds. Three-quarters of all couples, polling has shown, want to get married at different times—and the typical disparity is not a few days, but a whole season or two. He wants February, when football is out of the way. She wants October, when Fall foliage, roaring fires, and red wine provide for a romantic honeymoon. Most couples eventually compromise on June. No one knows why.

Type of Ceremony

Many couples choose a religious ceremony, in the belief that getting married in a church or synagogue will somehow atone for sins committed during courtship. Unfortunately, it doesn't work this way. If God has it in for you (and He probably does) He will view your stroll down the aisle as the worst kind of tokenism. If you are Catholic, God will be particularly displeased by your hypocrisy, since it's likely you stopped going to Mass years ago. Catholics caught in this bind should immediately go to Confession, or risk being hit by lightning on their honeymoon. Putting an extra hundred dollars in the Sunday envelope can't but help too.

You may want a civil ceremony, presided over by a justice of the peace, someone whose full-time job doesn't pay enough. With a JP, you can get married in a city hall, on a beach, in your own backyard, or for that matter, on a street corner. Some couples think it's groovy to get married on a hillside at dawn. Trust that it's not. Your friends will hate you forever for making them get up that early, climb that high, and battle that many bugs. And what kind of wedding reception starts at seven in the morning?

Flowers

The list is endless: the bride's bouquet; the bridesmaids' bouquets; corsages for mothers of the bride and groom; boutonnieres for the groom and ushers; flowers for the altar, if you have one; flowers for the tables at the reception. You will not believe how soon the flowers will wilt. You will not believe how much this will cost. Farmers in Argentina and Hawaii, where many of the more exotic blooms are grown, are laughing at you right now from behind the wheels of their Mercedes-Benzes. Thanks to you, they'll pay for *their* children's weddings in cash.

Some people think it's groovy to pick flowers from their own gardens or use wildflowers as an alternative to florists' arrangements. It isn't. It's cheap. And your friends will know it. We suggest that you forgo that do-it-yourself plan, keeping in mind that one of the goals of a successful wedding is giving your friends and in-laws as little post-event ammunition as possible.

What happens, say, twenty-five years down the line, when the offspring of two of these "liberated" couples decide to tie the knot? What if Mary Howe-Long marries Peter Willet-Waite? Do they become Mr. and Mrs. Howe-Long-Willett-Waite? Or do they do the wise thing: under cloak of darkness, sneak over to their parents' houses with matches and gasoline?

Either keep your own names, or go the traditional route.

Lame Name Game

Along with deciding where to get married, you should figure out what your married names will be. This is a relatively new step in planning a wedding. At one time, a man married a woman, she took his name, and that was that. No more. Although it is rare that a man will take a woman's name, some sadly misguided couples create new names to celebrate their union. Sally Cooke marries Sam Bacon, for example, and from then on they are known as Mr. and Mrs. Cooke-Bacon. Sally's cousin, Norma Frye, marries Sam's brother Ken, becoming Mr. and Mrs. Frye-Bacon. You see how ridiculous this is.

But wait! It gets worst!

Bridal Party

The bridal party consists of: the maid of honor, ordinarily a still-single woman who will be made miserable by yet another friend's wedding; the best man, ordinarily a brother whose childhood preoccupation was inflicting noogies on the groom; bridesmaids, a group of six to eight women, at least one of whom can't stand any of the others; ushers, whose job is looking ill at ease in rented clothing; ring bearers and flower girls, undisciplined brats who would tear the church apart if not given something to occupy their time.

The father of the bride's responsibility is to "give the bride away," which is another way of saying get her the hell out of the house once and for all. Tradition has not been kind to the mother of the bride, who has no formal role except to stand around lamenting how little elasticity she has left in her skin. Even more useless are the groom's parents, whose only input into the proceedings is picking up the tab for the rehearsal dinner.

Attire

The bride

The traditional bridal outfit is a gown whose price tag could only be justified by the inclusion of four tires, a V-8 engine, and leather upholstery. You think that's a joke. You think it's ridiculous to spend thousands of dollars on something you will wear exactly once in your life. You obviously haven't gone shopping for your gown yet.

An entire industry has sprung up around outfitting brides, an industry that will exploit your joy for its profit. You will, no doubt, select your gown from a bridal shop, or from the bridal department of a large store. Be warned that these places employ middle-aged women who resemble your mother, women who will dab at their eyes as you emerge from the dressing room in an $8,500 wedding gown and say, "I'm sorry. It's just that you look so beautiful." This trans-

lates into: "I'm sorry. It's just that I was thinking of my commission."

The groom

You need a tuxedo. Beyond this, your best guide is what *not* to get. Anything polyester is unwise since it is flammable, and you can count on the fact that at least one drunken guest at the reception will brush against you with a large lit cigar. Sherbet shades are a no-no. So are velvet lapels, unless your job is warming up for Wayne Newton.

The mothers

The mother of the bride gets to choose her dress first. Then it's up to the mother of the groom. Consultation between the parties is recommended, the thinking being that showing up at the chapel in the same dress could precipitate war. It has; specifically the First World War. As historians know, Francis Ferdinand, Archduke of Austria, was not assassinated because of some significant geopolitical dispute. It was because Ferdinand's mother and mother-in-law, contemptuous of prewedding consultation, showed up in identical dresses.

Rehearsal Dinner

Since this is the only part of a traditional wedding for which the groom's parents foot the bill, this is the only opportunity to achieve some sort of in-law equity. The rehearsal dinner is a golden opportunity to soak the old duffs with a fancy restaurant, an elaborate menu, champagne and wine. Although it is possible to really run up the tab with only the wedding party in attendance, it may require too much creative ordering, eating, and tipping. A surefire way to achieve your goal is to invite distant relatives, neighbors, and if necessary, total strangers.

Your Vows

Vows are exchanged at every wedding. Although the words have been uttered millions of times, no one ever gets them right:

- ♥ You say "I do" when it's not your turn.
- ♥ You mispronounce your name.
- ♥ You mispronounce your spouse's name.
- ♥ You don't mispronounce anyone's name, because you're too terrified to pronounce anything.

There are two defenses against the embarrassment of fumbled vows. One is an extremely loud organist. The other is elopement. Two words about writing your own vows: forget it.

The Reception

The primary aim of a reception is to pay back all the social obligations your parents have accumulated over the years; this is why parents, not participants, pay. Another aim is to avoid drunken brawls between your families. In extreme cases, it may be advisable to hold two separate receptions in two separate cities on two separate dates for your two separate families. This may sound like a lot of trouble, but it's less than the alternative: postreception litigation.

Guest list

It's inevitable that you will forget someone. You can avoid this by making a list of everyone you have ever known and inviting them. Depending on how popular the two of you are, this list could well run into the thousands. That's okay. After all, you're not paying.

Invitations

You want something simple but elegant: black-ink serif script on linen paper; your partner wants to make a statement, perhaps with Day-Glo orange. You want just the facts: time, date, place; your partner wants something that reads as if Rod McKuen wrote it. What's *wrong* with your partner? Doesn't he or she know that people keep these things—mostly to laugh over?

Don't let them.

Location

The only people who should have outdoor wedding receptions are bedouins. These people, not you, live in tents.

Your reception *must* be indoors. Halls can be rented, including ones designed especially for this kind of large-scale event. CAUTION: Do not rent a facility that can accommodate two functions simultaneously. If you do, you can be assured that the other event on your wedding day will be an induction for the International Order of Middle-aged Men in Funny Hats. These people, who wear red fezzes and carry noisemakers, could soon tire of their event and crash yours.

Open bar?

Always. An unlimited quantity of free alcohol is important even if no one drinks; guaranteed, before it's all over, most of them will.

Menu

The standard wedding fare is chicken cordon bleu ("blue chicken") with side dishes of Italian green beans and Delmonico potatoes. All of these selections are traditionally overcooked (this does not necessarily mean warm), but on the low end of the price scale (this does not necessarily mean inexpensive). Why not break with tradition? Offer guests a choice of baked stuffed Maine lobster or filet mignon. Granted, this will double or triple the cost of the wedding, BUT REMEMBER: YOU'RE NOT PAYING.

Band

Music is an essential part of a wedding reception. It must be live. Using CDs, tapes, or disc jockeys is the musical equivalent of picking your own flowers. Bands range from the large and loud to the small and tasteful, and instruments range from electric to eclectic. Any band that suits your taste is fine, so long as you can get an agreement, in writing, that it will not play "Feelings" more than once.

Matchbooks

Technical schools advertise on matchbook covers. There's no need for you to.

Photographer

Remember that nerd in sixth grade who always sat in the back row picking his nose? The one you gave wedgies to? He grew up and became a wedding photographer: a *cheap* wedding photographer, which is why your parents will insist on hiring him. At the church, he will be in everyone's way. At the reception, he will be the field marshal, ordering your every move. He will develop your prints at Fotomat.

He will, in short, get his revenge.

But could you forgo the photos? No. Wedding photos are essential; they provide concrete proof that at one time in the distant past, he had hair and she wore a size eight.

Videotaping

Forget preserving the moment. Forget posterity and the lovely plans you might have to someday show your children and grandchildren how it all started. The fact that there is a popular television show that awards cash prizes for blooper videos is the only serious reason to tape your wedding.

Prenuptial Agreements

The statistics say that 50 percent of you will wind up divorced. It's best to know in advance whether you fall into that category, since it will determine, for example, how zealously you'll guard your beer-bottle collection and how aggressively you'll defend your rights to the lobster-pot coffee table.

Please answer the following True or False:

1. There are these teensy, weensy things about him/her that drive you crazy—he chews with his mouth open, for example, or she snorts when she laughs—but you're sure you'll learn to ignore them after your married.

2. Your doctoral dissertation was on the behavior of subatomic particles in superconductive lithium; your partner's plans for career advancement include buying into an electrolysis franchise.

"And do you both promise to
love, honor . . . and to obey
the prenuptial agreements?"

3. In the interest of economizing, your partner routinely reuses tea bags; your idea of sacrifice is settling for a BMW when your heart is set on a Porsche.

4. You consider yourself dressed up if your shirt has a collar; your partner's idea of fashion is dictated by the pages of *Vogue* or *Gentleman's Quarterly*.

5. Your favorite writer is William Safire and your partner uses words like "irregardless" and "undoubtably."

Two or more True answers means that if you still intend to go through with this unnatural act, you should have protection. That's called a prenuptial agreement. This document, typically drawn up by lawyers who have the souls of lab rats, should settle certain decisive questions. Among them:

1. Who gets the single copy of *Catcher in the Rye* that each of you swears you've had since junior high?
2. Who gets the *Eagles Greatest Hits* CD?
3. Who gets the Fred Flintstone jelly glasses?
4. Who gets the lava lamp that came with your apartment?

The operative principle here: Don't assume that just because you brought something into the marriage you get to take it out again.

The Wedding Thank-You

It's advisable to write thank-you notes in advance. This is possible since every couple in America receives, in identical numbers, the same wedding gifts. All you'll have to do later is fill in the names and stuff the envelopes.

What you'll get:

- ♥ Six cheese boards.
- ♥ Five bud vases.
- ♥ Three General Electric toaster ovens.
- ♥ Five silver-plated trays.
- ♥ Five sets of wineglasses.
- ♥ Two twenty-dollar savings bonds with a maturity date of 2040.
- ♥ Two sets of Tupperware bowls.
- ♥ One framed black velour "painting."
- ♥ Four sets of bath towels in four clashing colors.
- ♥ Four clocks, one of which is a cat whose tail ticks off the seconds.
- ♥ Three oddly shaped items whose identity and purpose will forever remain mysteries.

(Note: this is for a wedding of fifty guests; ten other gifts, mostly more cheese boards and bud vases, will trickle in during the year. For a wedding of 100, multiply by two; for 150, multiply by three, and so forth.)

Sample thank-you letters:

WHAT YOU WANT TO WRITE:
Dear Bob,
We are returning your toaster oven with the hope that you will, while still wet from showering, stick your fingers in it.

WHAT YOU SHOULD WRITE:
Dear Bob,
Thank you so much for the lovely gift.
It will have a special place in our home and remind us, always, of you.
Again, many thanks.

WHAT YOU WANT TO WRITE:
Dear Fred and Linda,
We give up. What the hell is that thing you gave us?

WHAT YOU SHOULD WRITE:
Dear Fred and Linda,
Thank you so much for the lovely gift.
It will have a special place in our home and remind us, always, of you.
Again, many thanks.

WHAT YOU WANT TO WRITE:
Dear Uncle John,
Can you believe it? Here we are, twenty-six and twenty-eight years of age, and we don't own a single clock! No wonder we're never on time.

WHAT YOU SHOULD WRITE:
Dear Uncle John,
Thank you so much for the lovely gift.
It will have a special place in our home and remind us, always, of you.
Again, many thanks.

WHAT YOU WANT TO WRITE:
Dear Aunt Joan,
We are returning this cheese board in the mail because, were you here in person, we'd be tempted to hit you with it.
P.S. You forgot to take the price tag off. At $6.95, yours was the cheapest.

WHAT YOU SHOULD WRITE:
Dear Aunt Joan,
Thank you so much for the lovely gift.
It will have a special place in our home and remind us, always, of you.
Again, many thanks.

WHAT YOU WANT TO WRITE:
Dear Sally,

A bud vase! How perfect! A gift almost as predictable and boring as you.

WHAT YOU SHOULD WRITE:
Dear Sally,

Thank you so much for the lovely gift.

It will have a special place in our home and remind us, always, of you.

Again, many thanks.

WHAT YOU WANT TO WRITE:
Dear Cousin Esther,

Thank you for the set of matching Tupperware bowls, all of which do, indeed, "burp."

WHAT YOU SHOULD WRITE:
Dear Cousin Esther,

Thank you so much for the lovely gift.

It will have a special place in our home and remind us, always, of you.

Again, many thanks.

"Wow! That's the first toaster-oven with table lamp and built-in clock radio I've ever seen."

Chapter 2

The Perfect(?) Honeymoon

The Limo

The official start of the honeymoon is when Aunt Flo has hokey-pokeyed herself into angina, and you, the happy couple, sneak upstairs to change. You come 'own. The band plays. Through a shower of rice, you run toward a motor vehicle. WARNING: Do not use your own car for the getaway. Your friends will have tied tin cans to the muffler and painted JUST MARRIED on the back window with shaving cream. The custom was cooked up by jealous single people with the sole intent of embarrassing those luckier than they. You want a limo, which comes with an armed chauffeur whose instructions are to detain anyone found in possession of shaving cream or tin cans. A limo also should come with champagne, chilled lobster, and a functioning time machine to freeze the moment, since things never get any better.

Behind you is the wedding, which, despite the great planning, anticipation, and excitement, was as nerve-racking as having the lead in your sixth-grade play. Ahead of you are bills, arguments, and worst of all, learning the true art of compromise. You don't know that yet. All you know is that soon you'll be in your hotel room. Alone. Finally.

The Wedding Night

There was a time when the wedding night was an evening of great discovery and thrill, when a couple joined hands, stepped to the edge of some great sensory cliff, and jumped off. Sometimes that still happens, although not nearly as often since Dr. Ruth got her own radio show.

Nowadays, the wedding night is usually when the carping about in-laws begins in earnest. The groom, for example, usually waits until the wedding night to confess that he hates the Yankees, which has been the bride's father's favorite team since childhood, and the supposedly shared love of whom has been the only thing the two have had in common. The bride swears that if their children look anything like his sisters, she'll drown them. (In most cases, she'd be wise to.)

The wedding night is also the time when guilt, which is the glue holding most marriages together, begins to be laid on in earnest. In a weak moment, she feels guilty over how much her parents paid for the wedding. In an even weaker moment, he feels guilty that he didn't insist his parents share the tab. She feels guilty that she refused to kiss him every time some moron clinked his glass. He feels guilty that his best man forgot to mention his new wife's name in the toast.

In other words, there is plenty of fodder for a medium-size quarrel, although usually not enough for the First Big Fight (see Chapter 3).

Typical Wedding-Night Conversation Number One:

She: You hesitated before you said "I do."
He: I was nervous.
She: You were reluctant.
He: I was not.
She: You were too.
He: Was not.
She: Were too.

Typical Wedding-Night Conversation Number Two:

She: You spent more time talking to your friends than me.
He: I was talking to everyone. I didn't ignore you.
She: Yes, you did.
He: No, I didn't.
She: Yes, you did.
He: No, I didn't.
She: Did too.
He: Did not.
She: Did too.

Habits

The wedding night is also when each of you realizes, with stunning finality, that those annoying quirks you discovered in your mate when you were merely going out aren't going away. Worse, now that you're legally wed, there's no need even to attempt to keep those habits and rituals under wraps. What judge ever granted a divorce for farting in bed?

Among the realizations:

♥ You'll be living the rest of your life with a man who wears socks to bed.

". . . and hon . . . you forgot to put the seat on the john down again!"

♥ Or with a woman who sleeps in her college T-shirt—an oversized, threadbare, shapeless expanse of cotton emblazoned with such clever slogans as "100 Years of Women on Top."

♥ He'll never stop grinding his teeth.

♥ She'll never stop talking, not even in her sleep.

♥ He'll insist on setting the alarm clock, whether there's anything to get up for or not.

♥ She'll make no disguise of putting her retainer in before going to bed.

♥ And he'll make no disguise of taking out his bridge.

♥ She can't get out of the bathroom in under half an hour, no matter what she's doing in there.

♥ He leaves his used Q-tips in full view on the sink.

Where to Honeymoon

All right. The wedding night is history, and you're off on your honeymoon. The greatest care and planning, we hope, went into these details. You only get one honeymoon. You do not, on your return, want to be saying, "Thank God it's over."

Fortunately, enterprising profit-seeking Americans have created dozens of so-called honeymoon spots coast to coast, places that specialize in honeymoon suites, hot tubs, romantic dining, and vibrating beds.

A Dozen Popular Honeymoon Spots

The Poconos
Where *everyone* is on his and her honeymoon. And where, after a week of heart-shaped tubs, heart-shaped beds, heart-shaped pools, and heart-shaped desserts, you'll be ready to rip the heart out of the person who created this whole heart-shaped monstrosity.

Cape Cod
Where everyone spends a daily average of three hours and ten minutes stuck in beach traffic.

San Francisco
Where everyone is required by local ordinance to ride a cable car, dine at Fisherman's Wharf, cross the Golden Gate Bridge, and listen to Tony Bennett's last almost-decent song.

Hawaii
Where everything costs twice what it does on the mainland,

"How romantic. Think of the hundreds
of other honeymooners who
have soaked in this hot tub."

and death by lava is a potential hazard.

Florida/the Caribbean
Where everyone has a better tan than you.

Europe
Where everyone is more sophisticated than you.

Las Vegas
Where everyone is richer than you.

Aspen
Where everyone is richer, thinner, and better looking than you.

New Jersey
Where you can tour large chemical plants and wastewater treatment centers, and ride on the nation's most fragrant turnpike.

Seattle
Where everyone claims to love

rain. And big trees. And rain. And salmon. And rain.

Niagara Falls

Where love tubs and mirrored ceilings are almost as plentiful as in the Poconos.

New York City

Where entertainment consists of watching Donald and Ivana being administered a daily beating in the gossip columns.

How to Get There

Many honeymooners prefer the automobile, which tends to be cheaper, and allows for extended freewheeling discourse on just what's wrong with his or her family. Unlike a train, plane, or boat, you do not have to wait for the privacy of your honeymoon suite to start calling one another names.

Despite sweeping changes in the roles of the sexes, what happens between married people inside an automobile remains rooted in the past. She may be a corporate vice-president, he her secretary, but behind the wheel, it's 1953 again. The groom, who uncomplainingly takes direction from his female boss, will refuse to trust his new wife's interpre-

tation of the map. The bride, who handles multimillion-dollar accounts, can't figure out the turnpike toll.

There are destinations, of course, for which air travel is more practical. Having watched news accounts of approximately 245 planes go down in the last year, including several piloted by men who routinely consume nineteen rum and colas half an hour before flight time, you may no longer believe air travel is a smart idea. But jets are actually safer than cars, except when there's trouble. When there's trouble in a car, you pull over and call Triple-A. When there's trouble in a plane, you immediately plummet thirty-two thousand feet, landing in a Midwest cornfield in the form of pieces no larger than one of the beer nuts they serve when things are going better on your 767.

You may want to consider trains as an alternative. Train travel is widely considered romantic. This myth has been perpetrated by people who have never set foot on a train. Rail passengers can expect beautiful unfolding panoramas, friendly service, and toilets that were last cleaned in 1974. That's assuming you can fit inside a train "bathroom," whose basic model was copied from a communal bathroom at a Viet Cong prisoner-of-war camp. Most passenger trains in this country are run by Amtrak, which, you may have noted, is a misspelling. That should tell you something about passenger-rail service in Amerika.

What to Do on Your Honeymoon

Aside from the obvious, there are an almost limitless number of things to do on your honeymoon. You can sight-see. You can go to a movie. You can visit a museum. You can play miniature golf. You can play tennis. You can play shuffleboard. You can gamble. You can lounge by the hotel pool. You can sit in a sauna. You can go shopping. You can catch up on your reading. You can go to a nightclub.

If all else fails, you can visit the local emergency room.

Why?

Assuming you have health insurance, admission is free, which is more than can be said for miniature golf. You can also be sure that the beds will be freshly made with clean linen, which is probably more than can be said for your motel. But the greatest appeal of an emergency room is that the staff will give you its undivided attention, which is more than can be said for your spouse.

Depending on where you honeymoon, drinking the local water will get you into an ER. So will eating the local delicacy, usually something that grew somewhere you would never dare set foot. So will spraining your ankle trying to impress your spouse on the tennis court. Or getting a bad case of poison ivy.

On your honeymoon, you can also visit tourist traps, where the main entertainment is making fun of the tourists. Here's a perfect chance to "remember" ("get back at") the friends who gave you such lovely wedding gifts. Depending on where you are, you might want to consider buying miniature models of the Golden Gate Bridge, miniature models of the Statue of Liberty, miniature models of the Eiffel Tower, miniature models of the Washington Monument, miniature tombstones of those crazy fools who went over Niagara Falls in barrels, or the ever-popular plastic lobster.

Tourist attractions

On Cape Cod, a popular tourist-type attraction is whale watching. If the idea of bus-sized mammals spewing dirty water from "blowholes" ("gross anatomical parts") sounds like fun, this is for you. The fact that captains of whale-watching vessels are there because they can't find respectable work on, say, licensed tankers or freighters shouldn't dissuade you.

In New York City, a stroll through Central Park is highly recommended, assuming you like litter, loiterers, and stagnant, feather-filled water (the exact same water, still unchanged, used to fill these "ponds" more than 130 years ago, when Frederick Law Olmsted designed the park). Central Park is one of the few remaining places in America where you can, in broad daylight, watch a drug deal go down. Or a priest being mugged. Or a grandmother having her purse snatched.

In Florida, you can roast. This is true no matter where you go in the "sunshine" ("too much" sunshine) state. Better yet, you can watch the locals, 41 percent of whom were born before the state was admitted to the union. Being in Florida is like being on the set of *Cocoon*. Picture your grandmother in Lycra. Picture Granddad on roller skates. Picture what's happening out there on the roads. People as old as time still have their driver's licenses.

The Permanent Record

You will want to videotape your honeymoon and, perhaps, take still photographs for a scrapbook. This record will come in handy when, usually within a year, you do not have the money to go to McDonald's, never mind away for two weeks. Do not, however, think that your friends will want to see snapshots of you two in the hot tub. Love may be blind, but they're not.

Intimacy

There is the notion that the best spontaneous sex between a couple occurs on the honeymoon. This was last true when your parents got married. If you are like most newlyweds, your best spontaneous sex has already happened. This doesn't mean that things have to go downhill. Now is the time to start getting creative, to confess your innermost fantasies and begin to act them out. Why not pretend that you're characters from one of Shakespeare's plays? That you're famous movie stars—Gable and

Lombard, say? That you're stranded on a desert island?

That you're barnyard animals on a farm in Iowa?

Postcards

Postcards, whose chief purpose is to allow you to gloat, are an indispensable part of your honeymoon. You should send them early, often, and to everyone, except to people you forgot to invite to the wedding. No matter what is actually happening between you, the message should be relentlessly upbeat. Excessive use of exclamation points is advised.

Example:
It's rained all week.
You write:
"Getting a fabulous tan, drinking piña coladas by the pool, taking in all the sights!!!!!!!!!"

Example:
The honeymoon suite is smaller than your car.
You write:
"Talk about cozy!!!!! Talk about love nests!!!!!!! Danielle Steele couldn't have done better!!!!!!"

Example:
The airline lost your luggage, the restaurant rejected your MasterCard, the rental car broke down, and the honeymoon suite inadvertently was given to someone else.
You write:
"What a trip!!!!!!!! What adventure!!!!!!! Wish it could last forever!!!!!!!!"

♥ *Chapter 3* ♥

Talk's Not Cheap

Communication can be the oil that greases the marital gears. It can also be the monkey wrench. Except for learning how to manipulate with guilt (explained below), mastering the art of communication is the most important task facing you as newlyweds. Herewith some guides:

Saying 'I Love You'

This is the newlywed's most useful phrase. Whereas before marriage, "I love you" means "I love you," after, it can be used in almost any context, including:

♥ "I love you. And I'm really sorry but I just ran over the dog."

♥ "I love you. By the way, my mother seems to think she's invited for a two-week visit." (See Chapter 5.)

♥ "I love you. You don't think spilling Sprite on the VCR will ruin it, do you?"

♥ "I love you. So does Morris, which must be why he sprayed your shoes."

The First Big Fight

One watershed event in the life of newlyweds is that day when affection is replaced by naked aggression, which quickly escalates into the marital equivalent of thermonuclear war. You are having your First Big Fight. This

"And then I said
Bla . . . Bla . . . Bla . . . Bla . . .
Bla . . . Bla . . . Bla . . ."

"I told her
Blah . . . Blah . . . Blah . . .
Blah . . ."

". . . Are you listening to me?"

should be no cause for alarm. Every newlywed couple has one; the sooner it's over, the sooner you can move on to the Second Big Fight, Third Big Fight, and on through an open-ended series. Neither of you will win the First Big Fight, but the skills acquired during it could help you to victory in the second.

Question: In all likelihood, which topic will spark the First Big Fight?

A. The issue of parental consent for teenage abortions.
B. The validity of the Battered Woman Defense.
C. Right to die: morally, is there one?
D. Dirty underwear.

Answer: D.

Research shows that the first Big Fight usually happens within three days of the end of the honeymoon and usually concerns the undergarments that one of you left on the bathroom floor. Although dirty underwear can easily be laundered, it must first be transported to a washing machine, which, as newlyweds, you probably don't own. Addressing that issue often precipitates the Second Big Fight.

To wit:
He: It's your turn for the Laundromat.
She: I went last time.

He: No, you didn't.
She: Yes, I did.
He: No, you didn't.
She: Yes, I did.
He: I always go.
She: No, you don't.
He: Yes, I do.
She: No, you don't.
He: Yes, I do.
She: I promise I'll go next time.
He: You won't.
She: I will.
He: You won't.
She: I hate you.
He: I hate you too.

Caution: Do not throw objects during Big Fights.
This is not out of concern for your spouse's safety and well-being, since, during a Big Fight, no sight would give you greater pleasure than watching the EMTs take him or her out the door on a stretcher. You should not throw objects because some of them will break. Lamps, for example. With your luck, the lamp you throw will be the one your mother-in-law gave you, along with some long song-and-dance about how this particular lamp has been In The Family for sixteen generations, how no price tag can be attached to it, how it was handed down to her by her favorite grandmother, etc. Your mother-in-law will immediately notice the missing lamp on her next visit, assuming you are not clever enough to have found a

way to keep her out of your place for good.

Cheese boards do not break, at least not until you run them through the dishwasher or chop them into stove lengths for use in the fireplace. They can be thrown with impunity.

Although there's no foolproof way to get over your First Big Fight, sex, at least this early in the game, usually works. If it doesn't, you might want to consider a Major Purchase. A new Miata, for example, will soothe most ruffled feathers, at least until the first day both of you want to take it to work.

Caution: Do not mistake a Major Tiff for a Big Fight.

An example of a Major Tiff is when she was supposed to get Orville Redenbacher's Cheese-flavored Microwave Popcorn, his favorite, and came home with Pillsbury's Cheese-flavored instead. He says: "That's all right, honey" (translation: "thank God I didn't trust you with the beer, you twit"), then proceeds to sulk all the way through his Mets game. Those experiencing a Major Tiff do not have the uncontrollable desire to hold a pillow over their spouse's head, although they usually wish they could take back their vows.

The Apology Note

Saying "I'm sorry" after a fight or tiff is one way to make up, but it's fraught with risk. While you may honestly believe you are about to apologize, your tongue may play a trick on you at the very last moment. "I'm sorry, dear," can too easily become "Go to hell, you moron." Writing a note can avoid this unpleasantness, since, if your hand starts to play games, you can start over without penalty.

Example of acceptable apology note:
Dear ——:
I'm so terribly sorry I told everybody at the party about your toupee. I'm so ashamed of myself. Can you ever forgive me?
P.S. And I know I should never have pulled it off and let the dog play with it. I promise I'll never do anything like that again.
Love,

Example of unacceptable apology note:
Dear ——:
I'm sorry, I mean, I guess I am. Except that I really think you're the one who should be apologizing, since you started the whole thing. Which was

really pretty lousy of you, considering how I always understand when you forget something. And I still don't think it was that big a deal that I drove off with your keys on the front seat of my car. I mean, what were they doing there in the first place?

Delivering the apology note can be troublesome. You do not want to deliver it in person, since the same demon that might have played games with your tongue might cause you to spit in your spouse's face. Leaving it taped to the refrigerator is the preferred option, since, at least in hot weather, refrigerator condensation will cause the ink to run, leaving the note indecipherable. This is exactly what you want; the drawback to the apology note is that it provides a permanent record of who apologized first, something that will be used against you in the future.

Hidden Agendas

Within the context of a marriage, words take on strange new meanings. Sometimes, you'll be able to figure them out.

What he says:
"Not tonight, dear, I'm too tired."

What he means:
"Not tonight, dear, I'm too tired."

What she says:
"Not tonight, dear, I'm too tired."
What she means:
"Not tonight, dear, you repulse me."

What he says:
"You look unbelievably beautiful tonight."
What he means:
"When we get home, let's go right to bed."

What she says:
"My, what an interesting outfit!"
What she means:
"Did you dress in the dark?"

What she says:
"Of course I like your mother."
What she means:
"I can't stand the bitch."

What he says:
"Of course I like your mother."
What he means:
"I hate your mother too."

What she says:
"But I *love* all your friends."
What she means:
"Your friends suck."

What he says:
"Your friends are the best."
What he means:
"Are they *all* on Xanax?"

Danger!!!!! Never Bare Your Soul To Your Spouse!

You may be tempted, during your first year together, infused as you are with a sense of closeness—us against the world, them and us, two peas in a pod—to reveal certain things about yourself that you've never told anyone. What a relief it is! Such personal liberation! Finally, someone who won't shudder to know that until he got married, he was a regular customer of a telephone sex service! At last, a soul mate who nods understandingly when his wife confesses that in times of extreme stress, she still sucks her thumb!

If you cannot stifle the urge to confess, see a priest or, even better, your barber or hairdresser. You'll both be better off the sooner you understand, as all older married couples do, that today's sympathetic nod is tomorrow's slap in the face. Along with your poignant confession, you might as well hand your partner a loaded gun and say, "Here, the next time we have a Big Fight, pull the trigger." Because he or she will use this intensely private information against you in cruel and unusual—and usually quite public—ways:

—You'll be having a Minor Tiff in front of her parents when she'll say, ever so casually, "Honey, why don't you tell Mom and Dad about those 900 numbers you used to call? I'm sure they'd be interested."

—When playing charades, he'll walk around the living room with his thumb in his mouth. When everyone gives up, he'll say "my wife," then proceed to explain why.

—Knowing your lifelong struggle with a diet, she'll start bringing home chocolate cakes.

—Knowing your fear of insects, he'll "forget" to close the window that doesn't have a screen.

During such scenes, you will, at first, horrify yourself with your reactions. You will shred the section of the newspaper that he wanted to read, throw the pieces at him, and shriek, "Here, read this." You will sweep her favorite mug off the kitchen shelf and say, "Oops," as it shatters on the floor. You will tell him that you lied when you said he was good in bed, and that he's not nearly as good as the old boyfriend who's on Wall Street making millions. You will, with full knowledge of her hypochondria, say that such behavior clearly indicates the onset of neurological disintegration not unlike the course of premature Alzheimer's disease.

As your newlywed life continues, the horror will be replaced by the realization that the quicker you can acquire offensive skills, the quicker you can achieve parity in the relationship, or at least not be bullied to the point where it's always you writing the apology notes. The best long-term strategies incorporate the ability to stifle the urge to scream, along with a mastery of the sharp-tongued barb. Sharp-tongued barbs are designed for maximum damage, which means nothing whatsoever is sacred. The proper way to field a sharp-tongued barb is through the preemptive strike.

Example: Say, "Have you put on weight, or is it just my imagination?" before she can complain about you sitting down in front of the game again.

Example: Say, "Is that a double chin or is it just the way you're holding your head?" before he can complain about how long you took in the shower.

Women: the most effective ammunition includes remarks about his gut, his height, his hairline, his income, his sexual prowess, your old boyfriends (you should have at least ten), and various strangers who've cast admiring glances at you.

Men: sensitive areas for her include breast size, hip size, the implication that she has facial hair, the fact that all of your old girlfriends (there were twenty-five of them) were great looking and had summer and winter homes, and any suggestion that she has deviated more than three ounces from her ideal weight.

Lying

Telling lies is the absolute worst thing you can do as newlyweds, unless you're good at it, or it's about money. Still, there are situations in which the easiest way out is the traditional "white lie," which means "any lie you can get away with."

Study these examples to learn how to lie:

Case Number One

You say you'll be home for dinner, but you run into an old friend, and one beer leads to another, which leads to another, which leads to another. You come in at midnight, half in the bag. You have forgotten to telephone. Your spouse has already called your mother and the state police.

—Stupid Lie:

"I was just about to walk out

the door when the boss asked me if the report was ready, and it wasn't, and, well, you wouldn't want me to lose my job, now would you . . . ?" This lie is particularly stupid if you are slurring.

—Smart Lie:

"Honey, I'm so sorry, I was just about to walk out the door when the boss walked up to hand me a bonus, and then insisted on taking me out for a drink, and, well, how could I say no, and then when we got there, he wouldn't let me out of his sight, and he's going through a divorce and so *he* didn't have anyone to call, and, well, you know, I didn't want to make him look bad. . . ." If you don't have enough money in a bank account to cover the "bonus," make sure you take out a loan, in your name only, first thing next morning.

Note: Smart lies always begin with a term of endearment, such as "honey," "dear," or "darling."

Case Number Two

You've promised you'll never smoke again, although that's the last promise you intend to keep. Usually, you can hide it with mouthwash and room deodorant. Tonight, however, you come home from work smelling like you've not only been smoking

cigarettes, but eating them too.

—Stupid Lie:

"Smoke? What smoke?"

—Smart Lie:

"God, honey, I feel so bad. It was only one, just one lousy cigarette, but you're right: I'm so weak, so despicable. I'm such a slime. I'm no good. I'll move out tonight if you want me to. But if you'll have me, I swear on our relationship I'll never, ever smoke again."

(Note: Lies that play on pity are particularly effective.)

Case Number Three

You are on a very tight budget. And yet you have been itching to make some major purchase: She wants the $120 dress from Talbot's, for example, or he wants the $84 loafers from L.L. Bean. In a weak moment, out of earshot of your partner, you call the 800 number and place your order. Two days later, realizing what you've done, you call back to cancel. Too late. Your order's on the way. In fact, when you get home that night, it's there. And your spouse was the first one home.

—Stupid Lie:

"There must be some mistake. I can't imagine how they got my name, or our American Express number, or the address, or phone number, or knew my taste in clothes/shoes. I think our best bet is to call the attorney general, don't you?"

—Smart Lie:

"Honey, it was the dumbest, most compulsive, stupid, shortsighted, selfish thing I ever did. I'm sending it back. In fact, I've already called to arrange it."

This lie is particularly clever, since, by tomorrow morning, your mate almost certainly will soften and let you keep your dress/loafers.

Guilt

You do not have to be Jewish or Irish Catholic to use guilt in marriage creatively, although it gives you a decided edge. With a little thought, you can learn how to manipulate your loved one with guilt. Manipulation through guilt is the art of making him feel bad by telling him he shouldn't in a way that lets him know he should. The goal

The Offending Act	The Guilt-Producing Reply
She forgets your birthday.*	"No, it's okay. Really. I have another one next year."
He breaks your great-grandmother's heirloom vase.	"Oh, don't worry. It's only been in the family for two hundred years."
She puts a dent in your brand-new car.	"That's all right, dear. Insurance will cover it, even if they'll never be able to match the paint."
He's out of town overnight on a business trip and doesn't call.	"I wasn't lonely at all. Honest, I wasn't."

*Forgotten birthdays are typically worth presents with a cash value of five hundred dollars or better.

of manipulation through guilt is a solemn vow to change behavior, or the promise of an expensive present.

Remember that tone and expression are everything. For example: It is your one-month anniversary, a momentous occasion in newlywed life, and you were planning a great night out. That morning, he tells you he'll be working late. Saying, "Oh, don't worry about it," only counts if you sigh softly before and after, and, perhaps, let your voice break before you finish your sentence. It doesn't work if you narrow your eyes, bare your teeth, and hiss out the words.

Telephone Communication

Before marriage, your phone conversations were long, soft, delicious affairs, peppered with pet names and crackling with excitement. As newlyweds, there will still be some of that, but you will gradually notice change, particularly in telephone conversations during which one or both spouses is at work. Before you can no longer claim status as newlyweds, your work-time phone conversations will have been reduced to something very much like this:

She: Hi.
He: What's up?
She: Not much.
He: Same here.
She: Dinner tonight?
He: Pizza.
She: Pepper and sausage?
He: How long have you known me?
She: Can you get it?
He: Yeah.
She: We need milk too.
He: Okay.
She: What time?
He: Regular time.
She: That it?
He: Yeah.
She: Bye.
He: Bye.

♥ *Chapter 4* ♥

Housekeeping

The Newlywed Apartment

Unless your last name is Du Pont, you will not be able to afford to live where you'd like. In fact, for some number of years you'll be totally embarrassed by the place you call home. You will go to any lengths to keep your parents, family, and friends away. This is not because your place is a pigsty (although that is a distinct possibility); it is because it has the approximate square-footage of a Quarter-Pounder box. What's worse, you won't even have the money to buy it.

Worse yet, as your newlywed life goes on, you will find that your already small place is getting smaller. Not in any pyschological sense, but in actual, measurable decrements. Stud-

ies have calibrated the shrinkage rate at approximately 7 percent a month. If you do not find a larger place by your first anniversary, you will find your "home" has become roughly the size of a tuna-fish can. Despite this, your rent will have tripled.

Apartment hunting is a challenge, but one you can meet, provided you understand the game. Your first step is to get the classified advertising section of your local newspaper, where you will find ads written by people paid enormous salaries to disguise the truth.

Once you have selected the place you think you might want, the next step is to make an appointment with a real-estate agent ("crook with high-school diploma").

Real-estate agents will go to any lengths to secure your business. They will call you at all hours of the day and night. They will drive you from here to hell and back to look at a listing.

They will send you business cards and Christmas cards and offers for a free vacation in some glamour spot, such as Buffalo. In fact, about the only thing they won't do is listen to you. You'll tell them what you want to rent or buy, and how much you can afford to spend; they will try to convince you that with a little creative financing (not buying groceries for the full term of the lease, for example), you could swing the rent on a

What it says:	*What it means:*
"Cozy."	The size of a tuna can.
"Has character."	Has roaches.
"Artist's dream."	Everyone else's nightmare.
"Centrally located."	In a bad neighborhood.
"Light and airy."	Cracks in windows; holes in ceiling.
"Spacious."	If you're a cockroach.
"Affordable."	Not on *your* salaries.
"Quiet."	If you're hearing-impaired.
"Fully applianced."	Hot plate included.
"No pets."	Landlord shot the last tenant's dog.
"Carpeted."	In orange shag, with dark stains of suspicious origin.
"Security system."	Door has lock, peephole.
"Heat included."	Just enough to keep the pipes from freezing.

"Look at it this way . . . There is no room
to have the in-laws over."

town house with doorman, pool, and underground garage.

You must be strong. You must stick to your newlyweds' financial game plan, which is: get in over your head, but only to the point where your parents can still bail you out.

Furnishings

As pathetically small as it is, your new home must be furnished, preferably in better taste than your prenuptial digs. At the absolute minimum, this means no Red Sox pennants or batting helmets in a place of promi-

nence in the living room, assuming you were lucky enough to find a place with a living room.

Although virtually no furnishing is essential to single life, with the possible exception of the can opener and the plastic milk crate, newlyweds do well with certain basics.

They include:

A bed

Perhaps the biggest hoax to come out of the sixties is that the water bed is a superior way to sleep. The problem with water beds is not only the safety factor—i.e., that one penalty for the poorly manufactured water bed, as opposed to the defective box spring, is drowning. Or that after you have drowned, the leaking water will ruin the downstairs apartment, precipitating a lawsuit against your estate.

The problem is that, when filled, these things weigh as much as grown elephants. Despite manufacturers' assurances (DO NOT REMOVE TAG UNDER PENALTY OF LAW!), this is more than enough tonnage to collapse the average floor joist the instant two ordinary-sized people get into bed.

What you want in a bed is something soft enough to be comfortable, firm enough to offer support, and big enough to give you some stretching room—in other words, the same criteria you used in choosing your mate. We suggest a king-size bed, whose mattress is large enough to double as the dance floor at your reception. If you cannot afford this size, or if it cannot fit into your home, you will have to settle for something smaller. This is when you'll discover one of the harsher truths of marriage: namely, that beds are for sleeping as much as for anything else.

And a sleeping human being is not a nice creature; two together are even worse. They snore, they drool, they grind their teeth. They kick and flail and steal the covers. They make territorial claims, often with more belligerence than Argentina did when invading the Falkland Islands. Inevitably, one partner will prove more adroit at conquering the lion's share of the mattress; the other will awaken feeling as if Interstate 95 had been rerouted over his body.

The best way to ensure diplomatic behavior while sleeping on a small mattress is through mental discipline and training. Start by drawing, with fluorescent orange surveyor's spray paint, a line down the exact middle of the mattress. The line should be bright enough to be seen through any sheets you will be using. Next, establish a system of punishment for either spouse caught crossing the line, except during amorous or playful moments. Suggested punishments include:

- ♥ Sleeping on the floor for a week.
- ♥ Cleaning the cat's litter box for a month.
- ♥ Taking out the trash for a year.
- ♥ Reading Slim Whitman's autobiography.

A couch

Every newlywed dwelling should have a convertible sofa bed. This

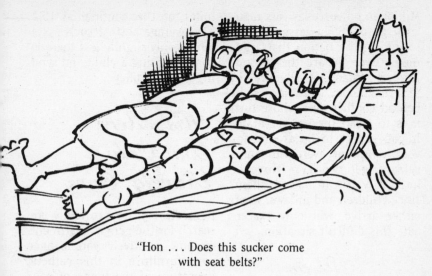

"Hon . . . Does this sucker come
with seat belts?"

modified medieval torture device doubles as a bed for his best friend, who drinks too much hard liquor to ever notice that the springs are large enough to be retrofitted into a truck chassis. Whether used or not, sofa beds should be opened and cleaned every six months. The popcorn and Cheese Doodles found during such cleaning should be saved and served to his best friend, who will not care how stale they are.

Tvs

Newlyweds do not need two checking accounts, two savings accounts, or even two ATM cards. But have two televisions or be prepared to fight, endlessly, over what's on the only one you own. This is true no matter how close you may be politically, philosophically, and religiously.

Examples of what can happen:

♥ She wants *The Simpsons*; he wants *Cosby*.
♥ She wants David Letterman; he wants Three Stooges reruns.
♥ She wants Tom Brokaw; he wants Dan Rather.
♥ She wants Wimbledon; he wants the Dodgers game.
♥ She wants a Woody Allen film; he wants Arnold Schwarzenegger.

Marriage counselors, whose highly paid work consists of methodically exploiting the misery of others, say every crisis can be worked through. Not true.

Millionaire divorce lawyers regularly go on Sally Jessy Raphaël to inform the nation that arguments over TV are the second-leading cause of divorce in America today, ranking right behind conflict over whose turn it is to clean the shower drain. If you expect to be around for your tenth, or even fifth anniversary, get two TVs—three or four if you can afford them, since children and in-laws, when either arrive, will only exacerbate this difficult situation.

Stereo

Most brides and grooms today each bring a seventeen-thousand-dollar stereo system into marriage. One stereo system can be dispensed with, since married couples soon spend 79 percent of their free time watching TV. Usually the stereo that should be sold is the husband's, which, having survived a frat house or bachelor apartment, has permanently sticky controls and food particles embedded in the speakers.

If neither bride nor groom has a stereo, you should get one. Purchased today, the complete stereo system includes CD player, tape deck, amplifier, tuner, equalizer, speakers, and a money-back guarantee that not a single component was manufactured anywhere within 1,500 miles of the continental USA. The average cost of such a system is only slightly less than the cost of raising a child and sending him to college.

His / Hers But Only Rarely: Ours

Regardless of how carefully you search for the perfect apartment, or how creatively you arrange your furniture in this pathetic caricature of the home of your dreams—or even if you *can* afford a twenty-four-thousand-square-foot house—the bottom line is, you will never again have Your Own Personal Space, something so vital to the single adult.

Before marriage, in the flush of true romance, it was all OURS. Marrying is like becoming guests of the Hezbollah; there's real danger your identity will slowly be obliterated. In marriage, even more than in Middle Eastern affairs, the concept of what's rightfully MINE becomes something worth waging holy war for.

Indeed, as newlyweds you will begin to defend your turf with the same jolly good humor as minks defending their young—however humble that turf may be.

You will amaze yourself with how aggressively You claim ownership of:

♥ Your toothbrush.
♥ Your coffee mug.
♥ Your shelf in the medicine cabinet.
♥ Your spot on the couch.
♥ Your side of the bed.
♥ Your place at the table.
♥ Your favorite wineglass.
♥ Your breakfast cereal.

But not everything becomes MINE. It is unlikely that you will claim responsibility for, or even admit the existence of:

♥ Dental floss found on the bathroom sink.
♥ The pile of toenail clippings that suddenly appeared on the night table.
♥ The spare change, dust kitties, gum wads, M&M's, sour-cream-and-onion potato chips, and mismatched athletic socks that inhabit their own shadowy worlds behind the stereo.
♥ The suspiciously pubic-looking hair that somehow wound up on the bathroom faucet.

Kitchen

Newlyweds do not spend most of their waking hours in the bathroom, living room, or even bedroom, as you may have been led to believe. They spend them in the kitchen. Kitchens are tricky places. With thought and care, they can be the bright and cheery heart of your happy new life together, redolent with spices and the aroma of home-cooked food. They can also degenerate into the enclosed equivalent of the county landfill.

Successful newlyweds are aware of kitchen pitfalls—and how to avoid them:

Dirty dishes

Get a dishwasher. This rule is inviolable. You do not want your marriage to descend to the level of arguing over an egg-encrusted fork. Without automation, it will.

The refrigerator

Refrigerators nowadays are sold with built-in spores, which means that no matter how tidy you think you are, leftover food will soon support a healthy growth of mold. This is why you need a pet, specifically a dog. Dogs will eat anything.

Refrigerators should be kept stocked according to the Newlywed Formula. In the lower compartment, you should have:

1. Six one-liter bottles of Diet Coke.
2. Shriveled remains of one hamburger casserole.
3. One half wedge of cheddar cheese.
4. One untouched, unidentified souplike substance, in a Tupperware bowl. This was a "housewarming" gift from the guy upstairs, whom you strongly suspect is a sociopath.
5. Two six-packs of Budweiser.
6. Three pounds of butter pats, which her mother scrounged from the reception hall when the wedding was over.

According to the Newlywed Formula, the freezer should contain:

1. Four bags of French fries.
2. Four packages of microwavable fried chicken.
3. Four D-size batteries, which his father-in-law insists last longer in cold storage.
4. The groom's wedding boutonniere, in a plastic baggie.
5. A slice of your wedding cake, in a plastic baggie.

WARNING: Never take your wedding cake out. It is to be eaten only in the case of a natural disaster—a hurricane or earthquake, for example—when the rest of your food is gone.

Tupperware

Names on all marriage licenses are fed into a national computer, which sends hourly updates over a dedicated line to the headquarters of Tupperware and Publishers' Clearinghouse. Receiving mail from the latter is no problem, since there is significant pleasure associated with holding a match to a smiling photograph of Ed McMahon.

Unfortunately, Tupperware cannot be burned. Within one month of your wedding, you will be contacted by a Tupperware hostess intent on having you sponsor a Tupperware party at which you and your guests will play games and all receive a free gift, such as plastic paper clips or a clear plastic sewing kit that "burps." There is no way to override this computer, set up and permanently funded under the sixteenth president, John Tupper. Similarly, there is no defense against Tupperware hostesses, all of whom honed their interpersonal skills during six months' training in the Iraqidesert.

Taking out the trash

Equality of the sexes, achieved after one of the great battles of

"We could blast!"

the sixties and seventies, does not extend to garbage. Women, who went so far as to fight for the right to see combat, did not fight for the right to take out the trash. Nor did men force the issue on this traditional responsibility, which began with Neanderthal woman threatening to withhold sex from Neanderthal man if he didn't remove the woolly-mammoth bones from the cave. The sooner the newlywed man realizes nothing has changed in this regard, the better off both newlyweds will be.

Bathroom

This is one place in the house where your slovenly habits will catch up with (and possibly even infect) you. Slimy soap and dirty bowls doth not a romance make. And unfortunately, there are no bathroom equivalents to the dishwasher and the trash compactor; cleanup is still in its primitive, i.e., strictly manual, stage. The only question is: whose hands are going to go inside the toilet bowl?

Unlike the clear-cut rule surrounding trash removal, there are no guidelines for cleaning the bathroom. You will think it small-minded and awful to argue over the chore, but not for long. Soon, you'll do anything to avoid it. Your best bet is to either clean together or hire someone to do it for you.

Roaches and Other Friends

Since they are still so close to single status, a stage of life when the concept of tidiness is defined as the absence of known pathogens, newlyweds tend to be careless with leftover food, vacuuming, and dirty dishes. Bugs know this. Any time a newlywed couple establishes a residence, it's like taking out a full-page ad in *BUG Today* that lists your address and has explicit directions, plus a toll-free number in case anybody gets lost. Within a week of moving in, roaches, earwigs, spiders, silverfish, and ants will take up residence with you if you do not move quickly.

The best thing to do is bomb. Bombing consists of closing windows and doors, removing all pets, then setting off hundreds of aerosol cans containing DDT, a carcinogenic pesticide available at low cost at your neighborhood hardware store. Bombing does not actually kill bugs, which, thanks to their ability to undergo complex evolutionary changes in under fifteen minutes, have developed resistance to every pesticide man has ever developed. But bombing will drive most bugs through the walls into your neighbors' apartments, where they will happily party until your neighbors bomb you in return.

Automobiles

Some couples bring only one car to a marriage. Others bring two. Ideally, they are the same model, make, and year. The danger of having two unequal cars (a new BMW and used Hyundai, for example) is similar to that of having radically different CD collections, namely that you will argue endlessly. What makes the car inequity more frightening is the comparative danger of running someone over with a Hyundai Excel compared with, say, picking up and throwing an entire CD collection at the offending spouse.

Applying for a Mortgage

Eventually, you will seriously contemplate buying your own house or condo.

Try not to.

Thanks to lending practices that routinely included loaning millions of dollars to anyone who could spell the word "develop," banks now find themselves struggling to pay quarterly interest on passbook savings accounts with $25.62 on deposit. Banks now want serious collateral on your mortgage, such as legal title to your first three children and every penny your parents have saved over the last four decades.

Sticking needles in your eyes is more enjoyable than applying for a mortgage, a process that takes twelve days and requires you to fill out 245 forms, all in triplicate. If you insist, come to the bank with plenty of food and water and a battery of well-rehearsed lies. Never state your true income, since, for most of you, hearing this figure will cause the bank officer to collapse in convulsions of laughter. On income, an exaggeration factor of at least five is recommended. You will, of course, have to explain this income in nonverifiable terms: family trust accounts, for example. To be most convincing, consider taking the name of a Saudi oil sheikh and wearing a turban.

♥ *Chapter 5* ♥

In-Laws

There is nothing you can do to make your in-laws like you, aside from having grandchildren (and even then, let's face it, it's not you they're fond of). They may talk politely to your face, but be assured that behind your back they are building little altars with Coke bottles and photos of you, through which they are sticking pins. Similarly, there is nothing you can do to make yourself like them, unless it is to arrange to deport them to some third-world nation not served by any major airline.

Mother-in-Law

Although there are more jokes about them than almost anything else, there is precious little amusement to be found in real-life mothers-in-law. His and hers are equally unpleasant, although for different reasons.

His deals exclusively in guilt, reminding him at every available opportunity that SHE SUFFERED GIVING BIRTH TO HIM and so should be honored all the days of her life. As far as his mother is concerned, he should call her as often as possible, inquire as to her health regularly, give presents to her on *his* birthday because IF IT WEREN'T FOR HER HE WOULDN'T BE HERE. If he doesn't dote on Mom (even if he never has), it will be your fault, you miserable bitch.

Just as he can never be good enough to her (especially since HE OWES HER EVERYTHING), you, the daughter-in-law, will never be good enough for him. Your cooking will give him ulcers, your nagging will give him migraines, and God help

"I know that Frank misses my cooking.
This should last until I bring more."

the poor boy the way you spend his money.

Her mother has the corner on the snobbery market. She'll wonder where you went to school, why it wasn't Harvard, and if by chance it was, why you were never invited to join Porcellian. She'll let you know that her daughter's last boyfriend—the one who came from that lovely (read: rich) family and is doing so well now at IBM (read: richer), what with all the stock options the company's offering him—is still available. And still handsome. And still has all his hair.

She'll let you know, ever so politely, that she can't understand why her daughter chose *you,* saying things like, "So, Richard, just what is it that a shop teacher *does*?" or "I understand, Thomas, that you really enjoy operating a forklift. Do tell us *all* about it." If you miss the irony of her comments, she'll think you an even bigger fool.

She will call you only by your

given name, even if it's Irving and the rest of the world has known you as Biff since birth, and you will call her Mrs. Whatever. That's quite enough familiarity for her, thank you. She will never, ever ask you to call her Mom, nor should you ever presume to. (It's your own mother, your own flesh-and-blood WHO LABORED FOR FIFTEEN HOURS TO GIVE YOU LIFE, who should be called Mom, you wretched ingrate.)

God help you, by the way, if mother and daughter are close. This means that soon enough, your mother-in-law will know everything about you (even more than the credit bureau, see Chapter 7). She'll know that you pace the floor as you brush your teeth and that you can't sleep unless there's a light on in the house and that you have a

"Gosh John, Mother has been here for three days . . . isn't it time you took her bags to the guest room?"

pet name for your genitalia. She'll know all this because her daughter will tell her. This may explain why, at family gatherings, you'll catch her glancing at you and shaking her head in disgust.

The bottom line is that, regardless of what you do or how hard you try, you will never be good enough. Your tie will never be straight enough, your paycheck never big enough, and just what is it your father does, anyway? Your wife's mother is, and will always be, as cold as rain on a January morning.

And about as enjoyable.

Father-in-Law

This is the benign subspecies of in-law, one that rarely causes any trouble. Observe three simple rules, and you'll do just fine: don't sit in his favorite chair, don't drink the last drop of his favorite Scotch, and don't take his favorite section of the Sunday paper before he's read it. Communication is pretty straightforward: a comment about sports, an observation about the weather, a snort of disgust about rising interest rates and declining stock prices is about as far into things as you and your father-in-law ever need to go.

Occasionally there are problems with the bride's dad. He may think you're some kind of no-good lug who wants to run off with his Little Girl. But even if you've ridden your Harley across his front lawn and pulled his Little Girl out the door by her hair, he'll be easy to win over.

Do what monkeys do when they're trying to minimize aggression: mirror his behavior. Examples:

The patriot
"Damn right," you say when he gets going again about those communists who are burning the flag.

The yachtsman
Sadly agree, "Bloody shame," when he, yet again, bemoans the loss of the America's Cup to Australia in 1983.

The baseball fan
Slap him on the back and say "How 'bout it, big guy?" when he enthuses over the Cubs' latest win.

The dweeb
Wrinkle your brow and say, "I too am confused by the entire concept of intergeophyscial exploration of the recombinant DNA structure found after the artificial infusion of cross currents of varying voltages," when

he puzzles aloud over problems at the lab.

Do this for a week or two, and you'll be best buddies. WARNING: Don't do it so well or so thoroughly that you actually begin to ACT like your father-in-law unless you want your wife to start acting like your daughter. The psychological implications of such a union are complex and troubling.

You, the bride, will almost always get along well with your father-in-law. You are younger, thinner, and better looking than his own wife, and far more pleasant to be around. He appreciates all of this and will show his appreciation by defending you every time your mother-in-law talks about what an odious creature you are (which, of course, will only make things worse).

Mostly, fathers-in-law are good for telling mothers-in-law to leave you two alone.

Brother-in-Law

Chances are good that you and your brother-in-law will get along just fine. You represent no threat to him, nor he to you. The only exception is if you are a short, balding man with a paunch and your brother-in-law is constantly mistaken for Tom Cruise. You will think you look so bad by comparison (and make no mistake—you do) that you will avoid him at all costs.

Otherwise, you two will exchange the occasional joke, share the occasional beer, sit in front of the TV at every holiday gathering, and hope no one taps you to do the dishes. WARNING: Do not let this amicable relationship lull you into telling him what you *really* think of your mother-in-law. She is, after all, his mother, and he's honor-bound to defend her.

Sister-in-Law

Things can get a bit contentious between the bride and her husband's sisters, especially if you all could be cast in "Beauty and the Beast," with you-know-whos as the you-know-whats. An easy remedy is to compliment the ugly ducklings lavishly and insincerely, and to constantly put yourself down. (WARNING: A compliment does not include remarking that you love their outfits, where *did* they manage to find such cute things in that size?)

Husbands, please note that it is tacky to hit on your sister-in-law. She *will* tell your wife, who *will* punish you for it for the rest of your life. As she well should.

In-Law Quiz

There are numerous ways to manage in-laws, some of them even legal. So put down the Uzi (be honest: could you really shoot his mother? Of course you could) and pick up a pencil. Test your in-law etiquette.

1. God knows why, but you are having your in-laws to dinner. Since, as newlyweds, your place has no single room larger than an elevator, you must split everyone up. You decide to:

A. Seat his relatives in the kitchen, hers at the coffee table set up in the living room.
B. Seat her relatives in the kitchen, his at the coffee table set up in the living room.
C. Seat older in-laws from both camps in the kitchen, younger in-laws at the coffee table set up in the living room.
D. Eat out.
E. Feign dual cases of hepatitis A, and cancel at the last minute.

Correct answer:
Although D has its virtues— it keeps everybody out of your place, and there's even the chance that the in-laws will pick up the tab, E is the hands-down winner. The point isn't just to keep them out of your home but, as much as is possible, to keep them out of your lives.

2. You're back from your honeymoon approximately fourteen minutes when the phone rings. It's your mother-in-law, popping the Big Question. So when are you gonna have kids, anyway?

A. Probably within a year.
B. As soon as we can.
C. After we get settled into our new jobs.
D. Didn't we tell you? The baby's due in six months.
E. It's none of your damn business.

Correct answer:
Although E has its merits, go for shock value. The best answer is D.

3. It's early December and your thoughts have turned to Christmas and Hanukkah gifts. There are thirty-nine in-laws on your list. You decide to:

A. Meticulously determine their needs and desires, then spend days and days buying thirty-nine personalized gifts.
B. Get everyone subscriptions to *National Geographic*.
C. Get everyone tickets to a Yankees game.
D. Get everyone nothing.
E. Have one of you schedule elective surgery for the last week of December.

While D is tempting, ignoring Christmas or Hanukkah will come back to haunt you, probably when the will to your wealthy uncle's estate is read. Choose E, which not only gets you off the hook, but gets you great sympathy too.

4. You've found the house of your dreams. There's no way you can afford the thirty-thousand-dollar down payment. Your in-laws offer to give you the money. You:

A. Decline the offer graciously, insisting that you two want to make it on your own.

B. Decline the offer graciously, knowing that if you accept, you'll owe them for the rest of your lives.

C. Accept the offer but insist on a repayment plan.

D. Accept the offer but insist on looking for a bigger place—one with room for your in-laws.

E. Forget eternal guilt, payment plans, and in-law apartments. Take the money and run.

Correct answer:
E, you selfish toad.

Holidays

Things really heat up around national holidays, which include Thanksgiving, Christmas, and at least in their judgment, mothers' birthdays. Certain critical decisions regarding holidays should be made well in advance:

Where to celebrate?

The best place is as far from where your families plan to gather as possible—preferably seven hours or more by air. You will need passports, advance tickets, inoculations, hotel reservations, time off from work, and thousands of dollars in cash. It's worth it. The longest-lasting marriages are those in which the couples have not attended a single in-law holiday gathering.

If you cannot afford to get away, go to any lengths to avoid having the in-laws at your place. You do not want your name directly associated with the bickering, complaining, sniping about food, and gossiping about who-wore-what that inevitably characterizes an in-law gathering. If subtle hinting doesn't keep them away, tell everyone about the recently discovered radon levels in your place, stressing that they have been scientifically calculated to be the equivalent of smoking six packs of cigarettes a day for 175 years.

What to bring

Okay. You've tried everything, but still you're roped in. You're going THERE. It happens. Etiquette demands that you bring something, but not necessarily what you'd like: a blowgun with poison-tipped darts.

According to a recent national poll, these are the most common gifts brought to in-law gatherings:

1. Cheese and crackers, arranged on a cheese board. "No need to return it," you will say, and you will mean it.
2. A bottle of wine costing less than five dollars, but with an elaborate multicolored label depicting an exotic flower and/or a majestic bird of prey in flight. As a rule of thumb, any bottle of wine worth more than five dollars you should keep for yourselves.
3. A dip with at least six ingredients, three of which are impossible to identify. Making a game of guessing is an effective way to disguise how bad the damn stuff tastes.
4. Something from your grocer's "bakery." Know that few things are as tacky as a cake, pie, or Italian pastry whose box has a bar code and is stamped with an expiration date.
5. Something from your grocer's freezer case. This is one thing as tacky as 4. Surely you can do better.
6. Something you baked. Unless you are on a par with Julia Child, think long and hard before bringing a delight from your own oven. Bad home-cooked desserts are often the subject of behind-the-back potshots for years and years to come. Better that you get something from the grocer's freezer case.
7. Nothing. *You* would never be so rude, but trust that when everyone's at your place, at least one free-loading in-law will arrive bearing this. You can put money on the probability that this mooch is significantly overweight.

How to eat

Regardless of what is served, always praise the cook. (Note: Never glorify the host of an in-law dinner gathering by referring to him or her as "the chef.") This rule is inviolable. Even if the turkey is burned so badly it looks as if it were recently extracted from one of the sealed reactor vessels at the Chernobyl nuclear power plant, do not comment about the color, texture, taste, or the fact that it glows when the lights are dimmed. Say: "Mmmmm! This is the best turkey I ever had, and you know how I *love* turkey!" If the peas are barely thawed or cooked so thoroughly that they turn to mush as they hit your plate—the peas, for God's sake!—say: "How *can* one microwave peas to such perfection!"

And if the cook has been particularly creative, foolishly venturing into culinary territory where only a Craig Claiborne would feel at home, say: "My, what an *exquisite* taste. Where *did* you get the recipe?"

In any case, you don't actually have to eat any of this stuff. Just remember a trick from childhood: secure the cook's creation in your jowls and politely excuse yourself from the table under the pretext of having to use the bathroom.

No matter how discreet you may fancy yourself, never return uneatable portions of food—chicken bones, for example, or olive pits—to your plate, since your mother-in-law has been watching you like a hawk throughout dinner and will later remark to friends and family how uncivilized you are and how

unbelievable it is a child of hers could have married such an unmannered beast. Uncomplainingly swallow all olive pits, bones, and strands of "the cook's" hair that you find in the salad or pasta. If the pieces are too large to swallow, excuse yourself to use the bathroom.

Conversation

The art of the in-law conversation consists of being witty and likable without revealing a single clue about how your new life together really is going. This requires great skill, since every one of your in-laws (with the exception of your father-in-law) believes it is his or her God-given duty to learn the facts, then spread them maliciously over the In-law Cooperative Telephone Network that spontaneously arises within three hours of announcing your engagement.

During dinner, the preferred topic of conversation is politics. The discussion will keep your in-laws at each other's throats and, one hopes, away from yours. Topics nearly equivalent to politics are abortion, the celibate priesthood, whether or not Elvis is really alive and well and living in Kalamazoo, whether or not Lee Harvey Oswald really shot JFK, and whether or not Dan

Quayle never uses his full first name because he can't spell it.

After dinner, there will be plenty of time to "catch up" on what everyone is doing. Your in-laws will break up into small groups isolated in different rooms so that they can gossip. Since your entrance into any of these cliques will bring immediate silence, the best way to really "catch up" is to eavesdrop. Among the things you will learn only by eavesdropping is that young Cousin Billy wasn't on hand today because he's back in reform school; that fifteen-year-old Cousin Missy got knocked up one week before her thirty-eight-year-old boyfriend split for L.A.; and that Uncle Paul has had so little to say because his latest rags-to-riches scheme, the local Kwik-Kleen rug-shampooing franchise, went under last week.

When to leave

As soon as you can.

There are no exceptions to this rule.

♥ *Chapter 6* ♥

Pets

Until you have children, pets are an essential ingredient of quality newlywed life. After you have children, pets are an essential ingredient of quality parenting, since shouting and screaming at them and locking them in the cellar presents fewer difficulties with the law than doing the same to your kids, who will deserve this treatment more than any poor animal.

Often, couples bring their own pets into a marriage. This can be nettlesome, since pets, like in-laws, have been deliberately bred over the years to automatically despise their masters' choice in mates. Different species have different ways of letting their displeasure be known. Dogs, especially the larger breeds, will probably attempt to rip your mate's arm or leg off. Cats, by nature more subtle, will express their sentiments by leaving a large sample of their own personal excrement on the side of the bed your partner prefers.

If neither of you has a pet, consider buying one as soon as you return from your honeymoon. But good luck agreeing on a single species. Men always want dogs; this is as instinctive to him as scratching his crotch when he thinks no one is watching. Women prefer softer, more cuddly animals, such as cats or untamed, underfed ferrets, which they can unleash when their mothers-in-law threaten to visit. Occasionally, compromise between newlyweds is possible. Some men, for instance, will agree to get a terrier, which is inherently a cat. Some women will agree to a Maine coon cat, which has the size and temperament of a pit bull.

For most couples, it is easier to get two pets.

Guide to choosing your pets

The circumstances of your new life together dictate what kind of pet is best suited for you. This quiz may help:

You live in a studio apartment in Greenwich Village, New York City, that's twice been broken into. You should get:

A. A French poodle.
B. Siamese cats.
C. A pair of finches.
D. The two largest rottweilers you can find.

Correct answer: D. Any time you plan to be away overnight, be sure to leave them without food.

You live in an old farmhouse in the Berkshires. You should get:

A. German shepherds.
B. A Jersey cow.
C. Rabbits.
D. An Appaloosa.

Correct answers: B, C, and D. It is a rule of country life that with the exception of barn cats and hunting dogs, pets should be edible.

You live in a condo in L.A. You should get:

A. A shar-pei.
B. A boa.

C. A macaw.
D. A Vietnamese potbellied pig.

Correct answer: B. You want a pet that makes a statement. And none make it more succinctly than a nine-foot-long reptile capable of swallowing small children whole.

Cats

Cats are independent, clean, intelligent, soulful, mysterious, regal, and soft enough to be kicked clear across a living room without hurting your foot. Only rarely, however, are cats effective mousers. They were in the old days, when every animal had to carry its own weight or have a skin that could be made into a human coat. But at the beginning of this century, cats across America called a congress and passed a unanimous resolution that henceforth, no cat would ever again work for a living. The boycott was successful. Not only do cats no longer participate in gainful employment, they have their own gourmet foods, television shows, cartoon strips, and swimwear calendars. Dogs could never be so ingenious, since intelligence for a dog is remembering how to stand up.

Apartment dwellers who get a cat will need a litter box. Enterprising humans have made huge fortunes coming up with new concoctions to fill litter boxes. Clay has gone into cat litter. Deodorant. Little green crystals. Perfumes. None of this is for the cat, who would be just as happy relieving himself on the couch, a practice in which it will happily engage the first weekend you're away. And no amount of little green crystals can mask the essential truth of the litter box: it gets full. And it starts to smell. And it needs to be cleaned, preferably sixteen times a day by the cleaning lady, doorman, or a visiting in-law.

The only thing more disgusting than the existence of a litter box is watching your pet use it. Which you will, since litter boxes always seem to end up in the bathroom, where all of *your* vital bodily functions except eating and sleeping are performed.

WARNING: CLAIMS THAT CATS HAVE BEEN TAUGHT TO USE TOILETS ARE FRAUDULENT! Such claims appear periodically in the *Weekly World News,* America's most accurate and meticulously researched publication, along with grainy black-and-white photographs of smug-looking felines crouched over the potty. Cats are too wise ever to be tiolet-trained, since it would deprive them of the supreme pleasure of watching their masters clean up after them.

The mouse drop is another way cats have fun at the expense of people. Although cats have long since been out of the business of mousing, they occasionally will, out of nostalgia and usually after ingestion of huge amounts of "catnip" ("cat reefer"), catch a mouse. After amusing itself for a half hour or so by "playing with" ("drawing blood from") the poor mouse, the cat takes a final, fatal bite. Remembering immediately why cats no longer go mousing, it will go into your kitchen and throw up on the floor.

Dogs

Dogs are loyal, but despite obedience schools run by people with phony British accents, it doesn't go much further than that. Sure, they can be taught simple tasks, such as swallowing and tipping over the water bowl, but don't expect a whole lot more. Aha! you say. This may well apply to golden retrievers, but don't certain breeds do better? The answer is no. Dogs may have a lot of fur or a skimpy coat. Dogs may or may not have tails. Dogs come in different sizes, colors, or weights, but the standard-model dog brain is no more complicated than the inside of a butternut squash.

When deciding what kind of

"Isn't that cute?
Old Barfo likes to sit on your pillow!"

dog to get, you will be faced with two choices: a mutt or a purebred. People from blueblood families prefer purebreds, which, like the families themselves, have long histories of inbreeding. Purebred dogs come with papers, officially stamped documents attesting to the fact that you've paid $1,500 for something you could have had free from the local animal shelter. Mutt is the abbreviated form of "mutant." The basic-model mutt is part collie, part shepherd, part Lab, part poodle, and part butternut squash.

Dogs are omnivorous. They will eat newspapers, shoes, chair legs, dirty diapers, plastic food wrappers, eggshells, coffee grounds, and absolutely anything you clean out of your refrigerator, no matter how long it's been there, or what color it's turned. But their favorite food is what's on your plate. You could sit at the table and pretend to dine heartily on cinder blocks and bricks, and your dog would still shamelessly beg. You could put one of the bricks on the floor, and he'd try to eat it. And probably succeed.

Residents of New York and other cities pay a price, worse than any tax, for having a dog. The price is called the pooper scooper, required—and this is no joke—by city ordinance. The pooper scooper is a concept designed to humiliate otherwise dignified human beings, since it requires the dog owner to become intimately acquainted with the animal's hour-by-hour gastrointestinal activities.

Rabbits

An acceptable compromise is rabbits, which are cuddly and cute and can be made into stew when the cuddliness and cuteness have worn off.

Aquaria

Tropical fish, which are highly colorful and incapable of scratching at the kitchen door before you're up in the morning, are a favorite of many newlyweds. A twenty-gallon tank is a tasteful addition to a living room and will, during the holidays, give visiting nieces and nephews an exciting new way to make Mountain Berry Kool-Aid. The basic aquarium setup includes a pump, filter, hood, purple light, heater, thermometer, gravel, plants, and giant snail, which you will have to shoot if it ever escapes.

What fish you put in your tank depends on what function you want your aquarium to fill. For simple viewing pleasure, angelfish and black mollies are recommended; hours of entertainment can be expected as the angelfish frantically tries to escape its tank mate, which considers angelfish fins a delicacy. An aquarium is also educational, providing a perfect forum in which to demonstrate the principles of the food chain. The food chain begins with the mother guppy, who swallows her young the instant they're born. It continues through the goldfish, which eats the mother guppy, and on to the catfish, which will consume the goldfish after it has died, bloated, come to the top, turned a sickening shade of yellow, and finally sunk to the bottom. The chain is complete when the giant snail eats the catfish and turns its attention to your cat, if you have one. Now is a good time to shoot the snail.

When the thrill of fish is gone, usually by the first fight over whose turn it is to clean the tank, animal experts recommend flushing them down a toilet. This is a highly humane practice. Tropical fish have been known to live up to ten years in sewers and septic systems—twice the average life expectancy in the wild, and at least thirty-five times longer than you can expect them to live in your tank, since neither of you will break down and clean it.

Birds

There is a reason the term "bird-brain" is a part of the vernacular. Birds make dogs look like graduates of Stanford. Let loose inside, they will fly straight into the mirror ("Look! Another room!") or the picture window ("Look! A bright sunny day!"). Let loose outside, they will fly away and freeze to death, if they don't get eaten first by the neighbor's cat. They do not come when called, cannot be trained to bring in the newspaper, and do not care if the bottom of their cage is covered with six inches of seed and excrement. They do not object to having a blanket placed over their cage at night. The only talented birds are certain parakeets and parrots, which can be taught to speak simple phrases. If you can get one to mutter obscenities in the presence of your mother-in-law, its overall stupidity should quickly be forgiven.

Exotica

In Brazil, many wealthy urbanites have lions. The word is that lions are useful in discouraging burglaries, but no one apparently has done any long-term studies comparing the disadvantage of being mauled with the advantage of not being robbed. Other exotic possibilities are tarantulas, leopards, lizards, monkeys, and pythons, which have significant economic value. Once he knows you give your pet python the run of the apartment, your landlord will be very forgiving when the rent is overdue.

The Vet

Vet is short for "veteran of charging outrageous prices." Most vets graduated from Harvard Business School, where they spent three years learning how to turn pet owners' worst fears into outrageous profits. Once upon a time, vets gave rabies shots, weighed the animal, scribbled in a chart, and charged twenty dollars. In recent years, to increase testing and treatment profits, they have invented a host of frightening new diseases, all of which are imaginary. Some they stole straight from real doctors, who *were* able to get into medical school: feline leukemia, for instance. Others were given the names of South American soccer stars: parvo virus being the best-known example. Still others were given acronyms: DCP-THG-12, which doesn't stand for anything.

"Is that you hon, or did you forget
to lock up the boa again?"

Vets also specialize in control of parasites through the medically sophisticated treatment known as "the bath and dip," or through the prescription of silver-dollar-size pills that can easily be gotten down the throat of any pet, providing you own a six-foot crowbar. Such measures are necessary because pets, especially cats and dogs, provide homes for creatures invented by the same people who scripted Japanese science-fiction movies in the 1950s.

One common parasite is the heartworm, which begins life as a larva ("disgusting white crawlie thing") small enough to be carried from place to place inside the blood of a mosquito. Once injected into an animal's skin, heartworm larvae, using navigational technology borrowed from the Patriot missile, immediately home in on the heart, where they take up residence inside the happy confines of a valve. The microscopic size of the larvae suggest that the adult ("even more disgusting white crawlie thing") heartworm should be no bigger than, say, a garter snake. In fact, adult heartworms fifty and sixty feet long have been removed during autopsies on dachshunds.

Another common parasite is

the tick. Ticks are insectlike creatures that, when dining, gorge themselves to six times their normal size. This is not unlike your sister-in-law. Unlike your sister-in-law, we hope, ticks drink blood and spread disease. The most notorious is Lyme disease, which turns its victims green and shrivels them to the size of a golf ball if left untreated.

Fleas are one of those remarkable organisms that have adaptive powers all out of proportion to their place on the evolutionary ladder. Enterprising flea scientists have demonstrated that fleas can jump 511,257 times their own height, which would be the equivalent of a human jumping from Syracuse to Toronto in a single bound. Fleas use this ability to get from the floor to your hair, where they immediately mate and begin the flea reproductive life cycle. The reproductive life cycle is approximately seventeen seconds, which means that almost before you begin to scratch, six million eggs have been laid and have hatched into fully grown fleas. The best defense against fleas is a flea collar, which you and your spouse should purchase in matching colors.

An alternative defense is getting rid of your pets, but no one ever does that.

♥ *Chapter 7* ♥

Finances

As newlyweds, you will learn that many things about you that were once appealing, or at least tolerable to your spouse, will become annoying. This holds particularly true in the area of finance.

Let's say that he used to describe you as madcap, spontaneous, and free-spirited. Let's say she used to call you levelheaded, practical, wise. Soon enough, you'll be flinging words like "cheapskate" at one another.

Some of it is that men and women basically view money differently: she sees it as money and he sees it as security. Some of it is that you are now sailing on the same financial ship, and that if one goes down, the other is going right along. And some of it is that you change when you're married. The man who wined and dined you with little regard for prices on bottles and less for the cost of a meal will turn into Ebenezer Scrooge. He'll carp about the cost of an appetizer and agonize over the price of the entrée.

The woman who used to buy you beautiful sweaters and silky ties will think better of spending her clothing budget on someone with as little regard for appearance as you.

The best thing to do is compromise, but you're married now, so that's out of the question. The second-best thing is to realize that you will never, ever have enough money regardless of how much you earn or how hard you try to scrimp and save. Once you accept this, you'll realize that it's pointless to worry about money. Better to just spend it.

Creatively.

Creative Financing

Many of you will be coming directly into marriage from high school, college, or home, all of which were financed by your parents. If they're like most parents, they set a terrible example for you. They paid their bills on time, deposited money regularly into a savings account, never charged anything that was ludicrously beyond their means. If they were crazy with money, they paid their bills early and didn't even have any credit cards. Remind yourselves that they were from a different generation and therefore couldn't help it, and vow not to repeat their mistakes.

Checks

Unlike real money, which has the United States government standing behind it, checks were never intended to be taken seriously. Any bank, especially new ones with names like "Bucks Я Us," will issue blank checks to anyone who can produce a high-school gym pass. At some banks, free microwave ovens or color TVs accompany the order.

Newlyweds can—and should—order checks by the thousands, and use them with little or no regard to the balance, an arbitrary, fluctuating number you do not ever need to know. Your balance is of concern only to bank accountants, whose idea of amusement is harassing you with unpleasant computer-generated letters.

Ordering checks is one of the first times, with the exception of the VD test needed for the marriage license, that your names will appear together on the same official-looking document. Unlike the syphilis test, you get to design this paperwork. Don't get carried away. You may choose color, size, typeface, ink, and background scene (not unlike decisions involved on your wedding invitations). You may be tempted by pastels and pictures wherein elves dance under mushrooms. DO NOT ORDER THESE. THEY WILL MAKE YOU LOOK STUPID.

When you bounce a check—and you will—get on the phone and lie. Tell your creditor that your dog has died, your mother is in the hospital, and your psychoanalyst has just unearthed the fact that you were abandoned as an infant. Let your voice break as you're telling the story, and at the end, cry softly. This ploy is particularly effective if the husband is the one making the call. Wrap things up by

promising that payment is on the way. You will have plenty of time. The thought of having to endure hearing you cry again will dissuade them from calling you for at least another year.

Note: this ploy has not been proven effective for amounts over one thousand dollars. For those amounts, a straight, no-nonsense talk, prefaced by mention of your close family ties to Saddam Hussein, is more effective. It can't hurt to refer to yourself in the third person as Commandant.

There are other ways to use checking accounts creatively. A successful financial strategy will employ all of them:

Grace periods

Take advantage of the fact that bills that arrive today don't make you liable for a late fee until weeks from tomorrow. Never mail a check until the day after your mailed statement says it's due.

Not signing checks

Make out your check meticulously, dotting every *i*, crossing every *t*, in penmanship that would do Sister Mary Ignatius proud. Then do not sign your check, thereby rendering it useless to your creditor and affording you an extra two weeks (or longer, depending upon what grade the clerk in the billing department completed) to come up with the necessary cash.

Not dating checks

Follow the above steps, this time leaving off the date, or filling in one that's off by several years.

Putting the wrong check in the wrong envelope

Send the electric company the check that's made out to the phone company and vice versa. Apologize profusely when each points out your error, and promise them the correct check is in the mail (see below).

Stapling checks to bills, wrapping checks around bills, folding bills, etc.

Useful if bills bear the standard "do not fold, staple, or mutilate" warning. This means that such bills are processed by computers that routinely spit out anything that deviates from their programmed format. Your check will end up on the desk of someone whose job it is to fol-low up on computer discards (in other words, someone with the IQ of lint). Count on an extra three weeks while this corporate Einstein figures out what your seven is doing with a line through it.

When all else fails, or when you've exhausted all of the above, there's always:

The check's in the mail.

Delivery is everything. It's important to sound earnest.

The check got lost in the mail.

The key here is to sound outraged that (a) the post office could actually *lose* something of yours and (b) your creditor could actually think you're *stalling*. I mean, really.

I'll send a new check in the mail (I swear).

Voice must contain throb of sincerity, edge of exasperation: how *could* this be happening to you? Derogatory comments about the postal service suggested.

The mail must be delayed.

Clipped, bored tone essential. This whole incident has taken up entirely too much of your time, and seeing as how it isn't your problem any longer—you did, after all, mail their check *twice*—you'd like not to be bothered again, thank you very much.

We'll drive the check over tomorrow morning.

Sound totally mortified and thoroughly apologetic. Ask what time the company opens, and promise you'll be there first thing.

The car broke down but we just handed the check to the mailman, who promises you'll get it by the end of the week.

Offer to put the mailman on the phone. Offer to get your spouse to vouch for your statement. Offer them your firstborn. The point is to avoid a late charge and, most particularly, a bad credit rating, which could be a major inconvenience when you apply for a mortgage (see Chapter 4).

College Loans

Should you pay back your college loan, or should you blow it off? Maybe you're thinking that of course you should pay it back, you promised to pay it back, a deal's a deal, your word is your word, and all the rest of that nonsense.

Answering the following questions may help put things in perspective.

1. Who comes first, you or Uncle Sam?

Correct answer: You.

2. Who needs the money more, you or Uncle Sam?

Correct answer: You.

3. Who suffered through four years of lectures on the decline and fall of the Roman Empire, only to find that no job interviewer ever asked you a single solitary question about ancient civilizations?

Correct answer: You.

4. So who deserves the money more, you or Uncle Sam?

Correct answer: Of course. You.

Don't worry. Senator Claiborne Pell of Rhode Island, the mega-wealthy sponsor of Pell grants, will pay for what you default on out of his own very deep pockets. The good senator can well afford it. He lives on the ocean in Newport, in the kind of house that has eighty-five rooms and a name. Maybe you'll even take a tour through his place on your honeymoon, in which case you should personally thank him.

Credit Cards

Through the mail, you will get fifty to one hundred unsolicited applications for credit cards. Apply for all of them; U.S. banking regulations guarantee you will get at least half.

Next, decide what you want to buy: maybe a new stereo, maybe a living-room set, maybe a wide-screen TV. Charge it. Decide what else you want to buy. Charge that too. Charge as much as you can, until a frowning clerk hands back your card and says "THIS HAS BEEN REJECTED," in a voice loud enough for the whole store to hear. This means you have exceeded your credit limit, an arbitrary number which has absolutely no connection to what you can afford. (If you could *afford* these things, you wouldn't be charging them, right?) Once your first card is "maxed out," you should pull out your second credit card. Charge up a storm until that too is "maxed out."

Continue in this fashion with credit cards three through ten. Use credit card eleven to pay off card one, card twelve to pay off card two, etc., until cards one through ten are paid off. You now have the option of using cards one through ten all over again, paying them off with cards twenty-one through thirty, or simply charging new items on the cards you haven't yet used. Keep paying off one credit card with another, an established practice known as revolving credit ("beating the system"). This, in essence, is how the Rockefellers built their fortune.

And if it's good enough for them, it should certainly be good enough for penniless sots like you.

If you're a little worried about the whole thing (more evidence of the truly horrible example your parents set), you should remember that your debt will probably never top more than fifty or sixty thousand dollars. This is peanuts. The S&L bail-out approaches half a trillion dollars and the interest on the federal debt in a second is more than yours will ever total in a lifetime.

Budget

Nonetheless, you will need a budget, if for nothing more than to help you decide whether you should spend most of your money on clothes this month, or blow it on dinners out.

Sample Monthly Budget:

Item	Expenditure
Chinese takeout	$236.80
Dinners out	$410.00
Lunches	$268.00
Breakfasts out	$124.30
Lean Cuisine	$63.45
Domino's Pizza	$56.00
Budweiser	$98.50
Häagen-Dazs	$54.40
Misc. food	$24.00
Pets	$60.00

CDs	$112.25
Video rentals	$84.75
Cable TV	$41.00
Book club	$38.30
Clothes	$300.00
Stuff for the house	$150.00
More stuff for the house	$50.00
Stuff for your cars	$50.00
Rent	$600.00
Electricity	$31.00
Telephone	$225.00
Savings	$15.00

COMBINED MONTHLY
EXPENSES: $3,092.75.
COMBINED MONTHLY
INCOME: $2,700.

You will note that your income does not meet your expenses. See CREDIT CARDS, above.

Controlling the Cash

"The world is his who has the money to go over it." So wrote Ralph Waldo Emerson more than a century ago. And guess what? Nothing's changed. In these days of equality, the balance of power still belongs to the person with the most money.

Wait a minute, you say. We're married now. Together for life.

What's hers is mine, what's mine is his.

Not for long.

Your money is your own, psychologically if not in actuality. Both of you know who earns more (don't underestimate the value of subtle reminders of this fact), and both of you know what that means: that he or she is the better person in the relationship. Inequities in earning can be offset by having a family with money—especially if that family shows any inclination toward sharing the wealth. Never let him forget that you wouldn't own a house if it weren't for the down payment from your grandmother. Never fail to remind her that your parents gave you a car as a wedding present and hers gave you a toaster oven.

The Myth of Marriage and Money

There exists the notion that two can live as cheaply as one. Just where this comes from is impossible to say—perhaps from the same single people who cooked up the idea of stringing tin cans from your bumper on your wedding day. In fact, as soon as you get married, you'll find the expo-

"Maybe if we put back the lobster meat
and the imported beer . . ."

nential factor kicks in, making it
eight times more expensive for
you to live together than it did
for you to live apart. This is
because each of you buys what
you want, plus what you think
the other wants, plus what each
of you thinks the other should
have.

Credit Bureaus

One of the truly exciting discoveries of newlywed life is the
credit bureau, which will, without being asked, become entan-
gled in any attempt on your part
to get a car loan, a mortgage, a

Visa card, or any other kind of credit, except personalized bank checks. Almost everything about the credit bureau, including its location, is a classified national secret; only the man who follows the president carrying that little black briefcase has authorization to reveal any detail.

Credit bureaus know everything about you and your spouse, including where you honeymooned and how many quarters you fed into the vibrating bed. No one has given the credit bureau permission to know any of this, of course, but they don't care. Like the CIA and Defense Intelligence Agency, the credit bureau uses wire taps, illegal electronic entry into banks' central computers, and surveillance to get the lowdown on you. There is probably a credit-bureau person in the tree outside your window right now.

The credit bureau is manned by the happy sorts of people who, in high-school biology class, volunteered to pith everyone else's frogs. You will never actually meet one of these people. You may, after days and days of messages left with a secretary whose personality has been surgically removed, get to speak to one over the telephone. Your conversation will go something like this:

You: "There seems to be an eensy-beensy error here on my credit report, sir. I never had an overdue amount on my First City Visa account. Sir, I have all the documentation on the account requested in your computer letter, including every monthly statement since the account was opened. A bad credit rating would ruin me for life. Could I please make an appointment to come in and straighten this out, sir?"

Credit-Bureau Person: "No."

Your next move logically would be to go to the credit bureau in person, probably armed with an assault rifle, except, as already noted, the locations of credit bureaus are closely guarded secrets. One week after your conversation, a dot-matrix letter will arrive in the mail. "Since you have refused to pay the overdue amount on your First City Visa account, said account is being turned over to our legal department for further action. You have seven days to respond. Be informed that under Chapter 1603.12 a. (c.), of the U.S. Code of Hammurabi, you have the right to dispute our finding. HA! SEE WHERE IT GETS YOU!" the highly personalized letter will read. In truth, all credit-bureau findings are final and become a permanent part of your "record." In extreme cases, they may wind up chiseled on your tombstone.

"Me . . . I thought you knew the passord."

Money Machines

The only idea more absurd than that money could grow on a tree is that it could come from a machine. Not surprisingly, the patent for automated tellers is held by two bank vice-presidents who, not so many years ago, locked themselves into the central vault and consumed massive quantities of LSD. Hidden inside early models of ATMs were illegal aliens, who counted and handed out the bills through the little door. Money machines are supposed to dispense only funds on deposit on your account, but this minor problem can be overcome by knowing the password for someone else's account. "Password," "money," and "machine" are the three most popular passwords.

Money machines, like Coke machines, are prone to frequent breakdown. Kicking them usually helps and, if the kick is strong enough, will result in thousands of free dollars, dispensed in crisp twenty dollar denominations. Timid machines will immediately cough up all their money at the first sight of a gun, although robbery is a form of creative financing only the most desperate newlyweds should consider.

Always Remember . . .

Spending money is a great way to forget your problems, even if those problems had to do with money in the first place. Odd, but true. There is no better cure for a big fat American Express bill than a good meal at an expensive restaurant.

Charged, of course.

Chapter 8

Leisure Activities

Something, perhaps an agent introduced into the champagne at the reception, permanently changes the way you and your new spouse approach your non-romantic spare time (for romance, see Chapter 9). Whereas before the wedding neither of you could get enough of the other's interests, after, what your spouse does in his or her spare time holds as much fascination for you as, say, whether or not the Big Bang theory is correct.

Consider his softball team. Men's softball is, in and of itself, an innocuous pastime. Eighteen men come together twice a week to drink beer, throw a ball, drink beer, hit a ball, drink beer, talk about old girlfriends, and drink beer. You, the new wife, will consider this a threat to your new union, as it excludes you, unless you volunteer to keep the beer cold. You should not. You should not endorse this behavior in any way. You do not want your husband to be reminded of his old girlfriends. You do not want him to drink this much beer. You do not want him to come home with seventeen of his sweaty friends.

Or consider ladies' night out. Clubbing is a favorite pastime of single women old enough—say, fourteen—to con their way into a local hot spot. Once inside, women drink a margarita, accept a dance, drink a black Russian, go to the ladies' room, drink a frozen strawberry daiquiri, refuse a dance, drink a white wine, use the telephone, drink a piña colada, and tell the Rick Moranis look-alikes who've been asking them to dance all night that if they were the last men on earth, the human race would grind to a halt.

Since any newlywed woman is bound to have unmarried friends who hop from club to club, she'll want to join them. Her new husband, naturally, won't understand. The smart newlywed woman will go out with her friends on his softball night.

Sports

The point of pursuing a sport is to hurt yourself. Sports injuries are wonderful ways to elicit pity, sympathy, and the occasional profession of scorn ("How could you let a ball hit you in the face? Don't you have any reflexes?") from your mate. And sports injuries are the best way to arrange an appointment with a sports-medicine specialist, the kind of doctor most qualified to prescribe bandages, whirlpool treatments, and Tylenol with codeine.

Nowadays, injuries such as broken ankles and jammed fingers are considered hopelessly old-fashioned; you need Carpal Tunnel Syndrome, or a Repetitive Stress Injury, or an Arthroscopic Subgeleal Glaucoma of the Right Quadrant Lattissimus. These are hard to diagnose, virtually impossible for a casual observer (i.e. your spouse) to challenge, and often chronic—meaning that you can milk the injury for all it's worth.

Health clubs

There is no better place to sustain a genuine sports injury than at a health club, since you can then sue the owner for millions in damages. Health-club owners carry humongous insurance policies to protect against just such suits, so don't be dissuaded by the notion that anyone will take this personally. Owners will be quick to settle out of court, which means you do not have to wait for a lengthy trial. There are three kinds of damages: "punitive," which means the owner will have to trade his late-model BMW for a Yugo; "actual," which must be paid in twenty dollar bills; and "critical," which is what your lawyer splits with the judge, in the rare event your case goes to trial.

Well-equipped health clubs have Nautilus, stationary bicycles, saunas, pools, racquetball courts, free weights, and indentured weights. They also have professional female staff members who paint their fingernails purple and whose every third word begins with the prefixes: "iso" or "like . . . um . . . wow." The best health clubs also have bars with wide-screen TVs turned to a twenty-four-hour sports channel, which you will be able to buy, along with your very own professional sports team, after your successful injury claim.

Sports you can play together

The advantage to certain sports is that they foster togetherness, keep you in shape, and let you go deeper into debt. For example, if you decide to take up cycling, you will have to buy two brand-new mountain bikes; the basic-model Schwinn in your parents' garage won't do. What you'll need is something lean and mean: something that weighs twenty-three ounces, costs $2,300, and will be completely ruined when it falls off the car bike rack you didn't have the right pliers to assemble.

Tennis
When playing doubles, make sure you're on opposite sides of the net; married teammates blame one another when they lose, which they usually do, since they spend more time arguing over broken serves than concentrating on their game.

Squash
Those of you intent on upward mobility need to know that this is more than a vegetable. Best you learn the sport together, thereby ensuring you won't embarrass yourself when your boss, a former champion, asks you to play.

Canoeing
Just the two of you, lost in a Hallmark moment as you gently paddle across a mirror-smooth lake. Until the speedboats arrive. And the jet skiers. And the water-skiers. And the blackflies. And dragonflies, the size of Huey helicopters.

Bowling
One of the rare sports in which participants can be overweight and out of shape, yet are encouraged to eat and drink while they play. The downside is those rental shoes. Have you ever really thought about who else has worn them? Or what might have been growing between their toes?

Friends

Take it as a given that he will hate her friends, and she will hate his. His buddies will be crude and lewd, the kind of men who consider Snap-On calendars high art; hers will be corporate VPs intent on careers. Or his will be cool and aloof, fond of discussing stock options and dropping names; hers will be neurotic and needy, dissatisfied with the hand life has dealt.

Ordinarily, putting together any two members of these groups and hoping for a romantic outcome is futile.

But occasionally, it looks like it might work. His best friend trades futures; hers is a vice-president of development at Merrill Lynch. His best friend races stockcars; hers owns a Harley. On paper, it sounds great. Inspired even. They'll be the couple you two will grow old with, the ones with whom you'll share summer vacations and holidays, the only family you'll ever let borrow your Weed-Wacker. Your children will marry one another. Perhaps, like the Kennedys and Fitzgeralds, this will be the beginning of a great American dynasty.

Forget it. PLAYING MATCHMAKER WITH YOUR FRIENDS IS LIKE PLAYING RUSSIAN ROULETTE WITH A BULLET IN EVERY CHAMBER.

Within five minutes of meeting, the two corporate types will be arguing over annuities; before you've even lit the charcoal for the introductory barbecue, the two motor enthusiasts will be challenging one another to a drag race on your lawn. Better that you leave the matchmaking to agencies with names like "Two-gether" or "Heavenly Buddies"—places that charge a fortune, ask clients to fill out detailed questionnaires, then make matches in the same scientific fashion with which straws are drawn from a hat.

Friends and Phones

Understand that he will hate the time you spend on the phone with your friends. Part of this is because he cannot comprehend what you possibly have to talk about, seeing as how you work together all week long and you've already talked once this morning. Part of it is because he's afraid that what you have to talk about is him. Part of it is because he's afraid that what you have to talk about isn't him. Poor boy. He'll never understand any of this, so don't even try to explain.

Men, you see, view the telephone as a utilitarian object, something whose sole purpose is to communicate information. Words are used as stingily as if the medium were Western Union.

Example of Men's Phone Conversation:

Joe: Frank. I got tickets to the game tonight.
Frank: Great.
Joe: Meet me at my place at six-thirty.
Frank: Okay.

Note that Frank didn't ask Joe where he got the tickets, how he got the tickets, or from whom. Note that he didn't thank Joe profusely or insist on paying for *exactly* his share of the evening. Note that neither exchanged such trivialities as "hello" or "how are you?" Note that neither asked the other what he would be wearing, who else might be there, how he was going to fix his hair, or whether this was the time and place to try out that great new hat.

This is how men converse on the phone, and there's little hope of changing them. Which is just fine. Imagine what it would be like if both of you were clamoring for a free line?

Entertaining

The primary purpose of entertaining is to invite friends to come over so that you may shamelessly gloat in front of them. (In-law entertainment is different, see Chapter 5.)

When having single friends over, gloating should be over your newlywed bliss, even if your First Big Fight erupted ten minutes before they walked through the door. Make sure that throughout the evening, you coo breathlessly, whisper sweet nothings, and blow kisses at each other, even if you'd

rather be slipping arsenic into your new mate's drink. Gloating over newlywed bliss is particularly effective if the invited single guests are recently divorced. Watch for their faces to light up with joy when you bring out the wedding album or insist on showing the video of your walk down the aisle.

Note: Gloating can be stretched out by showing each and every one of your wedding gifts. Make sure you leave the spare bedroom full of bud vases for last.

If your guests are married, the newlywed-bliss charade will quickly be exposed for what it is. This is because couples married for any period of time are remarkably adept at sensing underlying tension. You need a different tack with these veterans. The best one is to wait until you have just made a major purchase, over which you can shamelessly gloat. Wide-screen TVs, Italian leather couches, and Jacuzzis are acquisitions worth gloating over. If you cannot afford anything of this caliber (in other words, if you've yet to receive your charge cards), see if you can borrow something for an evening.

Since newlyweds are known to be feeling their way through domestic life, it is perfectly acceptable to solicit contributions when issuing a dinner-party invitation. With proper planning, all you need ever prepare at one of your own gatherings is the coffee.

Example:

You are having a dinner party for six, including yourselves. Ask Couple Number One to bring the main course, one side dish, and beer. Ask Couple Number Two to bring a different side dish, dessert, and wine. Be sure to set different arrival times, so nobody knows for sure that the sum total of *your* contribution was chilling the glasses and brewing the coffee.

The Party

Newlywed parties must have a degree of refinement lacking in the parties you gave as single people, when you would buy bags of pretzels and a half keg of beer and issue a general invitation to anyone whose last name had more than two letters. At a very minimum, vomiting should be discouraged at your newlywed party—at least inside. Your still-single friends should also understand that it is no longer acceptable for you to find them, naked and limbs entwined, unconscious on the bathroom floor the morning after the party.

The party menu

After five years of marriage, you will spend days preparing elaborate appetizers and hors d'oeuvres; after ten years, you will have the best caterer in town handle these details. Newlyweds needn't go to these lengths, but they must do better than pretzels and keg beer: bottled beer and deviled eggs, for example. If you feel like splurging, you could even buy napkins and plastic cups.

WARNING: NEVER HAVE SO-CALLED THEME PARTIES. THEY ARE INJURIOUS TO YOUR HEALTH AND REPUTATION.

There are two kinds of theme parties: those in which you expect your guests to humiliate themselves, and those in which you expect your guests to humiliate themselves, then buy something from you. A costume party is an example of the former. Usually (but not exclusively) held at Halloween, costume parties always feature one brilliant costume worthy of a Hollywood set and thirty-five last-minute, pathetic attempts at Casper the Ghost or Bonnie and Clyde. The other kind of theme party begins with homemade hors d'oeuvres, usually crackers and cheese (total cost: $2.85), and concludes with a high-intensity sales pitch for Tupperware, Avon, or House of Lloyd. Standing on a street corner with a tin cup is less humiliating for you—

and your guests—than this kind of shameless hucksterism.

Grocery Shopping

Making the list is the first thing you must do. Newlyweds, of course, are but a short step away from being single. Out of habit, many remain on the diets they believe helped them attract a spouse in the first place. Thus, their grocery list will be virtually identical to what it was when they were single. It will contain several kinds of fruits and vegetables, the leanest cuts of beef, generous amounts of fish and poultry, and high-fiber whole-grain breads and rolls. The list will be drawn up after consultation with calorie charts and health books.

The second you walk into the store, crumple up the list and make a beeline for the snack aisle.

Remember? You're married now! You don't have to eat carrot sticks and cottage cheese anymore! Those days are over, thank God! You and your spouse can guiltlessly fill your cart with Fritos, cheese popcorn, Chips Ahoy cookies, Sarah Lee cakes, Hostess Twinkies, Devil Dogs, Cheeze Whiz, Coke, root beer, frozen fried chicken, Reese's Pieces and Mars bars. For nostalgia's sake, you might want to throw in a bag of carrots or a tomato, but don't feel obliged to eat them. Consider them a colorful addition to the vegetable crisper.

Games

Sometimes—a rainy evening, for example—nothing fits the bill quite like games. They're fun, they're inexpensive, and they give you a chance to beat the pants off your spouse without laying a hand on him.

But, as with so many other aspects of newlywed life, discretion is advised.

Games newlyweds should play

Monopoly
For the next few years, this may well be the only real estate you'll be able to call your own.

Croquet
This aristocratic game is easy to learn, does not tax either body or mind, and can be played almost anywhere. Its chief virtue, however, is the opportunity it affords to drink unlimited numbers of gin and tonics while being eaten alive by mosquitoes.

Candyland

This game, designed for children, is about the least competitive and contentious game there is. Sometimes, that's just what you'll need.

Games newlyweds should not play

Solitaire

If it's come to this, the *two* of you are in deep trouble.

Strip poker

And if it's come to this, the two of you might as well just give up.

Nintendo

Nintendo is not a game. It is an obsession, if not an addiction, that brings out the absolute worst in people.

War

This game can too easily escalate into the real thing.

Family feud

So can this.

The Newlywed Game

Please.

Trivial Pursuit

Which is anything but. The only point of this insidious game, created by death-row sociopaths, is to point out your opponent's intellectual shortcomings. Played among friends, Trivial Pursuit can be bloody; between newlyweds, fatal.

Games newlyweds will play, like it or not

When's the light going off?

Bad enough that your spouse reads in bed. Worse that the light keeps you awake.

What's this charge?

Every monthly statement from every credit card you own will have a mystery charge. It's up to you to follow the clues and identify whose it was.

He: What's this lunch at Mama Basilesco's?

She: I thought it was yours.

He: I've never even heard of the place.

She: (Looking at calendar) I was home that day.

He: I ate at my desk.

She: It must be their mistake.

He: (Shrugs) Must be.

The only difference between this game played now and ten years down the road is that now you're too naive to suspect an affair.

Let's go to the movies

Once upon a time, a newlywed night out consisted of an early movie followed by a candlelit dinner. This was before the advent of the VCR and microwave oven, two technological innovations that spawned a new subspecies of human: the couch potato.

Newlyweds hardly ever go to the movies anymore, although contemplating it remains a favorite pastime.

He: Wanna go to the movies?
She: What's playing?
He: *Another 48 Hours, Robocop II, Die Hard 2, Delta Force 2, Young Guns II, The Two Jakes, Exorcist III, Rocky VIII,* and *Friday the 13th CLXVIII.* Any of that sound good?
She: No.
He: Let's rent something.

"What do you want to do tonight?"

♥ *Chapter 9* ♥

Romance

Romance during courtship is natural, unforced, exciting, and in certain states, in certain of its variations, illegal.

Once you're married—once everything has settled down and anything is legal—you have to work at keeping love alive. Newlyweds must pay particular attention to romance, or quicker than you can say "flannel nightgown," your relationship will become as exciting as rotating your tires. Your long-term goal should be to keep romance in full bloom over the course of thirty, forty, even fifty years; now is not too early to begin. Your short-term goal remains what it was before you tied the knot: preventing pregnancy, at least until you can afford something bigger than a studio apartment.

Setting the Mood

Spontaneity has a way of diminishing after you have lived with someone long enough to know his innermost secrets—the access code to his ATM account, for example, or how much she really weighs. Thankfully, there are countless tricks for newlyweds to kindle the sparks.

Wine

Wine remains Cupid's nectar, even if it now comes with sulfites, the chemical residue of what crows, sparrows, starlings, and common pigeons deposit on vines after a day of gorging themselves on sun-ripened grapes.

Like one's mate, wine must be

selected properly. Start by knowing when to choose white versus red wine. White wine is preferred for poultry, fish, and venison. Red wine is preferred by those couples who want to wake up after a long slow evening of romance with a pounding head. Unlike one's mate, the older the wine, in general, the better. Beware of wines so cheap they do not have a vintage on the label.

Champagne is the most romantic of all wines, what with its tiny bubbles and high price tag. The romance happens because it bypasses your stomach altogether and goes directly to your head, where it dampens inhibitions, heightens pleasure, and distorts vision to the point where even people fresh from changing the oil look irresistible.

Okay. So you don't know a Beaujolais from a bottle of Bud, and you suspect that pouilly-fuissé is some fancy French waiter's way of calling you a horse's ass. You don't know anything about nose or bouquet or finish, except that they don't have anything to do with what you're used to drinking. Don't despair. Follow our easy guide, and you'll soon be sniffing corks with the best of them.

As a general rule:

SAY NO TO: Any wine that has the name of an animal, such as Cold Duck or Wet Fish.

SAY YES TO: Any wine with three or more French-sounding words strung together, followed by a date at least a decade old. Example: Chateau Margaux Hemingway, 1975.

SAY NO TO: Any wine with the word "farm" in the title.

SAY YES TO: Wines made by religious orders. They've taken vows of poverty, fidelity, and chastity; you can be sure the one enjoyable thing left to them—booze—they do right.

SAY NO TO: Wine from any country that manufactures Yugos, exports Gabors, or is known for vampires.

SAY YES TO: Wine from France, California, New York, or Italy.

SAY NO TO: Any wine that is sold in a can, has a screw-off top, or comes in a bottle that could find new life as a yard-sale lamp.

SAY YES TO: Wine in a dust-covered bottle. Unlike other ingestible items—food comes to mind here—wine that has been sitting around in a cellar for, say, fifty years is considered a real treat.

Other liquid concoctions are equally conducive to romance. Amaretto is one popular choice, although not, one suspects, thanks to the ad campaign—whose sole purpose seems to be making you feel unsophisticated, unattractive, and ten years behind the times. Kahlua is another romantic possibility. Kahlua's label shows a little man slumped under his sombrero. You can well imagine what he just did.

Visuals

One way to set the mood for a romantic evening at home is the right film. This does not necessarily mean movies from your video shop's back room, although, if you're willing to degrade yourself by renting something with a title like *Vampire Sluts from Hell* from the sixteen-year-old clerk, it can. Perennial romantic favorites include *Romeo and Juliet*, *Casablanca*, *The Philadelphia Story*, and *It Happened One Night*.

Beware: There are films that set the wrong tone entirely, chronicling betrayal, separation, and serious bodily harm inflicted by jilted lovers wielding sharpened instruments.

Five movies not to rent

1. Fatal Attraction
Not likely to inspire confidence in marriage. Anne Archer is loving, kind, intelligent, and incredibly beautiful, and he still cheats on her.

2. Who's Afraid of Virginia Woolf?
A film that chronicles the dissolution of a tortured marriage. No need to know, yet, what might be ahead.

3. Gone With the Wind
He didn't give a damn, and she figured tomorrow was another day. What kind of relationship was that?

4. Gaslight
Don't give one another ideas.

5. The War of the Roses
The shame of it is, they start out young and happy and in love. Just like you. They get a little older, have a couple of kids, buy a great house. Just like you hope to. What happens next is too awful to contemplate. So don't.

Choosing the Food

The way to a man's heart, it is said, is through his stomach. In truth, the way to a man's heart is through his mother, who has probably spent much of her time during your courtship trying to keep him away from you (see Chapter 5). The right food, however, can't hurt.

Ten romantic foods

1. Oysters
In reality, these slimy, organ-shaped shellfish with the consistency of phlegm have no more romantic impact than, say, Richard Nixon. Popular culture holds otherwise. You decide.

2. French bread and Brie
The reasons for this should be obvious: Brie is creamy and smooth, French bread long and hard. Okay, so the symbolism is a bit heavy-handed. So, often, are the French, who came up with this combination.

3. Fresh strawberries
It's not for nothing that Hieronymus Bosch used strawberries as a symbol of orgasm. These plump and lovely fruits are perfect for feeding to one another. Slowly.

4. Whipped cream
Need more be said?

5. Chocolates
Sinfully rich, delightfully sweet. Just like your ideal mate.

6. Pheasant under glass
Have you ever seen this fabled dish? Neither has anyone else. But fairy tales are the stuff of romance.

7. Truffles
Fleshy, edible mushrooms with an exquisite flavor. As with all wild mushrooms, make sure someone else (your mother-in-law, for instance) does the taste testing first.

8. Lean Cuisine
Sometimes, fast *is* better.

9. Peeled grapes
If it was good enough for the ancients, it's good enough for you.

10. Steak tartare
Never underestimate the power of raw meat.

The Price of Love

After a while, it's going to take more than a phone call to make her heart pound, more than a card that says "missing you" to make sure he still does. One of the best ways to keep the fires of love burning is to buy things for one another. If such materialism makes you shudder, just remember that the boys who sang "Can't Buy Me Love" made enough money off the song to indeed buy love, and just about anything else their hearts desired.

The rituals of gift giving evolve throughout courtship and

"I read that sex burns about 400 calories."

marriage, becoming more expensive and less heartfelt as the relationship progresses. That's all right. The guiding philosophy of a marriage should be that any gift, under any circumstances, is better than no gift at all.

Dating

Her presents are carefully chosen and fraught with meaning; his are reflexive and repetitive. For example:

♥ She buys him a Cross pen and a box of Crane stationery because he's going away on a weeklong business trip.

He buys her flowers.

♥ She buys him a limited-edition print from the last America's Cup raced off Newport because once he said he liked twelve-meters.

He buys her flowers.

♥ She buys him a Braun coffeemaker and five pounds of handpicked fresh-ground gourmet beans because he always says she makes the best coffee he's ever tasted.

He buys her flowers.

Engagement

By now, you're secure enough in the relationship to begin trying to change one another.

♥ She buys him tickets to the ballet, a subscription to *GQ*, and the complete works of Shakespeare, bound in leather.
He buys her a bowling ball.

♥ She buys him flannel pants and Brooks Brothers shirts, hoping he'll throw away his threadbare corduroys and short-sleeved dress shirts.
He buys her anything from Frederick's of Hollywood.

♥ She buys him a membership to a health club.
He buys her *Jane Fonda's Workout* tape.

Marriage

The deal here is to either buy one another what *you* really want and excuse it by saying it's "for the house"—a new living-room set, for example, or a personal computer—or to just say, "Look, just let me know what you want, okay, because I have no idea what to get for your birthday."

Sweet Nothings

Probably by the time you're engaged, and certainly by the time you're married, the affection you show one another will alter substantially, i.e. she'll want more of it and he'll wonder what he can do to make it go away. He's never felt comfortable calling her "bunnykins" in front of anyone and he's always thought that moonlit strolls were overrated. She, on the other hand, loves being loved and wants constant reassurance and public declarations of that fact. This will be a source of arguments between you for the rest of your lives. You can avoid some of the problems by taking your cue from the following:

WRONG
She: Do you love me?
He: Yeah.

WRONG
She: Do you love me?
He: What do you think?

WRONG
She: Do you love me?
He: What kinda stupid question is that?

RIGHT
She: Do you love me?
He: I love you more than I ever thought I could love anyone. I love you more any man has ever loved any woman. My life would be worthless without

you. (Note: Do not finish the speech by saying, "All right? Are you satisfied now?")

WRONG
She: Did you miss me?
He: Yeah.

WRONG
She: Did you miss me?
He: When?

RIGHT
She: Did you miss me?
He: Miss you? *Miss* you? I was so unbearably lonely without you that I could barely think.

WRONG
She: Do I look okay?
He: Yeah.

WRONG
She: Do I look okay?
He: Why? You feel sick or something?

RIGHT
She: Do I look okay?
He: (Gasps) Your beauty takes my breath away.

WRONG
She: Is she pretty? (Question may refer to boss, co-worker, old girlfriend, friend's girlfriend, tennis instructor, dentist, or neighbor.)
He: Yeah.

WRONG
She: Is she pretty?
He: Compared to who?

RIGHT
She: Is she pretty?
He: Who, *her*? Are you *kidding*? She's a dog.

WRONG
She: Do you like my hair—?
He: AAARRGGGHHHH!!! WHAT HAPPENED TO YOUR HAIR?

RIGHT
She: Do you like my haircut?
He: I don't just like it. I *love* it! You look gorgeous!

Men, Take Note:

Much has been written about how your physical relationship changes after marriage, about how now that you don't have to seduce her, you won't. This is a losing strategy. She will be unhappy, and she will surely think of ways to spread her dissatisfaction around. Who can blame her? Try to remember that this is not a race, that the point is not to finish in time to watch the eleven o'clock news, that foreplay does not consist of yelling, "You got your clothes off yet?" from the bathroom.

If you're not sure how to act, just pretend this is your first date. Pretend you're trying to lure her into bed, instead of whipping in and out of it. Also, please know that standing in front of the mirror in sagging jockey shorts, flexing your biceps and saying, "Check this out, hon," is NOT seductive behavior.

Role Models

Many people believe that Romeo and Juliet pretty much had the last word in romance; modern times have produced no famous role-model lovers, at least not since Tracy and Hepburn. Nonetheless, this sorry state of affairs can be instructive, if only by giving you examples of the type of relationship you should go to great lengths not to emulate.

A dozen famous modern couples you DON'T want to model yourselves after

- ♥ Sonny and Cher
  The original, all-time couple from hell.
- ♥ Greg Allman and Cher
  Just when you thought it couldn't get any worse . . .
- ♥ Marilyn and Dan Quayle
  Poor Marilyn.

- ♥ Brigitte Nielsen and Sly Stallone
  Rocky meets his match.
- ♥ Brigitte Nielsen and Mark Gasteneau
  Rocky's match meets hers.
- ♥ Tammy and Jim
  The original, all-time couple going to hell.
- ♥ Chuck and Di
  How much more of them can anyone take?
- ♥ Pia Zadora and What's-his-name
  What is his name? And why should anyone care?
- ♥ Lee and Gary Hart
  There are no excuses for this kind of monkey business.
- ♥ Ronald and Nancy Reagan.
  You *can* be too thin and too rich. And calling your wife "Mommy" *is* downright creepy.
- ♥ Donald and Ivana
  Too much is, well, too much.
- ♥ Donald and Marla
  No excuses for them, either.

Where Romance Is Best

Once upon a time, *anyplace* (the beach, the backseat of the car,

the couch in your parents' basement) was right for romance. Those places still have potential but will lose some of their appeal as familiarity sets in (and as you realize how much more comfortable a bed is than a sand dune). Newlyweds must work to maintain the sense of excitement that accompanied their first encounters.

Experts say that one of the best ways to do this is to be creative, to discover new places to make love that will not get you arrested for indecent exposure.

GOOD IDEA: Your office, after hours.

BAD IDEA: Your office, after hours, if the cleaning crew comes in.

GOOD IDEA: The kitchen table, late at night.

BAD IDEA: The kitchen table, during dinner.

GOOD IDEA: Your backyard.

BAD IDEA: Your backyard, if you live in a condo.

GOOD IDEA: The car.

BAD IDEA: While it's moving.

BEST IDEA: In bed. That is, if you can stay awake long enough. One of the most shocking discoveries of newlywed life is that the waking hours you spend in bed will not necessarily be spent in wedded bliss. You will read in bed. Watch TV in bed. Eat in bed. Write letters, do your nails, talk on the phone, sort through mail. It doesn't mean things are over. It just means they, like you, are settling down.

♥ *Chapter 10* ♥

The Honeymoon's Over

There comes a time when you are, well, *married*. There's no surefire way to determine when you've reached this point, although using the bathroom without bothering to shut the door is a pretty good clue. Knowing when you've moved from "newlywed" to "recently married" status is important since it will allow you, for example, to pick at pieces of corn stuck between your teeth without having to excuse yourself from the table.

Generally, a common household scale can be used to gauge the end of the honeymoon period. Ten pounds of collective weight gain is well within the standard margin of error and cannot be used as a definitive point of demarcation. Thirty pounds, however, is a realistic threshold. Once you're passed that point, it is safe to have sec-

ond, and even third helpings of anything in sight.

Caution: Weight loss cannot be construed as a sign that the honeymoon has started up again. It can indicate parasitic infestation, some stress-related syndrome, or most probably, the start of an affair.

Some other signs

—The couch begins to look more attractive than your spouse.

And it is.

—The TV begins to seem like better company than your spouse.

And it is.

—You stop referring to your mother-in-law as "Jane" and start calling her "the bitch."

—He joins a second softball team.

—She'd rather clean behind the toilet than watch him play.

—He lets weekends pass without shaving.

—She does too.

—You win a contest, but can't decide whether to take the brand-new Electrolux or the weekend getaway package.

Baby Time

As reliable as other indicators may be, the only infallible sign that you have ceased to be newlyweds comes when your first child is born. For 40 percent of today's couples, that happens within six months of the wedding; of the remainder, 60 percent of newlywed wives are pregnant by the end of the first year of marriage. (The rate rises to 98 percent if your preferred method of birth control is the condom, which ranks just below withdrawal and prayer in effectiveness. Condoms are manufactured by firms whose labor-management relations are such that employees routinely bring straight pins to work.)

Women learn they are pregnant by throwing up. Men learn their wives are pregnant by discovering them throwing up. This is a moment of special closeness, filled with anticipation and unbounded joy.

Suspicions are confirmed by going to the local pharmacy and buying a home pregnancy kit, which consists of a shrink-wrapped card on which is printed a question: "Do you feel like shit?" A "yes" answer in this test, which is 99 percent accurate, indicates a positive result. Home pregnancy kits are generally displayed next to condoms, proof that druggists are not without a sense of humor.

Labor and delivery

For the father-to-be, watching his baby come into the world is one of life's most exhilarating experiences, ranking right up there with watching the application of conductive gel to the temples of a condemned man. Of course, it is no better for the mother-to-be. There is a widespread belief that pregnancy and childbirth are two of life's most gratifying experiences for women. This is a myth perpetuated by health-care professionals whose idea of entertainment is watching a good bullfight.

Eventually, the baby will be here. Under pressure to cut costs, today's hospitals allow you a stay of no more than thirty minutes after birth. This can be stretched to upward of a month by mentioning casually that you never wanted this baby and you intend to kill yourself and it at the first opportunity.

"Well Frank, either I have the flu . . .
or you're going to be a daddy!"

If you suffer a *true* mental lapse and decide to take the baby home, consideration must be given to your pets. Cats will be exceedingly jealous and will do anything to get rid of the new member of the family. Cats have been known to kidnap one-week-old humans and place ads in newspapers seeking outrageous ransoms for their return. They do not keep their word when the money is paid. Instead, they sell your child in a foreign country, usually South Korea, where American babies are much in demand. This, in fact, is where your cat probably spent his time while you were in the hospital— standing on some street corner in Seoul, bidding up the price on your baby.

Since dogs have only three brain cells, and since each is spoken for (chewing, swallowing, peeing), jealousy will not be within their capabilities. Most dogs, therefore, will form attachments to babies. This does not mean they will protect them.

Golden retrievers and other breeds with highly skewed brain-to-body-weight ratios have been known to hand over infants (and the entire contents of the family safe) for no more than a pat on the head.

What the expectant can expect

Your first baby will mark your transition from contentment to chronic sleep deprivation, a condition that will remain unchanged until every last one of your children has left home.

As much as you love this newborn treasure, as much as you marvel over the perfect being you two have created, you will soon realize that kids are an incredible amount of work. And that while the hard part of parenting older children is the psychological element, for now, it's all physical. A well-trained monkey could do it—something you might want to look into if the going gets particularly rough.

You will, in short order, come to resent those parts of parenting that rob you of your newlywed bliss: the feeding, the diapering, the feeding, the bathing, the feeding, the rocking, the feeding. The only things that babies do more than eat are spit up and cry.

To wit:

—You're just sitting down to a quiet dinner. The wine is chilled, the candles are lit and THE BABY STARTS TO CRY.

—You've finally rented a movie you've both been looking forward to. The popcorn is popped, the sodas are poured, and THE BABY STARTS TO CRY.

—You've both had a long week, but an easy meal and a good night's sleep will take care of everything. The pizza is hot, the beer is cold, and THE BABY STARTS TO CRY.

First Anniversary

Congratulations! You made it through your first year. You've had your ups and downs, good times and bad. You've started to really get to know each other. You're settling into a groove. You believe things will only get better, that you'll grow closer with each passing year, that great poets someday will pen tribute to your love.

Ha!

Marriage, start to finish, is a constant struggle. You must learn to compromise. You must learn to apologize. You must learn to grovel. Every time you get really angry at one another, every time

you feel the word "separation" on the tip of your tongue, remember all the wonderful times you've had together. Remember that anything worth having is worth working for. Remember how badly you can get soaked in divorce court, and that prenuptial agreements aren't worth the paper they're printed on.

But most important, remember that your spouse now knows enough about you to embarrass you for the rest of your life. Do you really want him out there on the loose? No. You want him by your side, for better or worse, for richer or poorer, in sickness and in health. At least that way, you can effectively practice damage control.

And maybe, at least once in a while, recapture the magic of being newlyweds.